with best wishes
from
Olof.Wijk.

December 1970.

Eat at Pleasure
Drink by Measure

Eat at Pleasure
Drink by Measure

Compiled and edited by
OLOF WIJK

Illustrated by Yvonne Skargon

CONSTABLE
LONDON

First published 1970
by Constable & Company Ltd
10 Orange Street
London WC2H 7EG

© copyright 1970 by Christopher & Co. Ltd.
94 Jermyn Street, London SW1

ISBN 0 09 457300 X

This book has been set in Monotype 10pt Baskerville, 2pt leaded,
with titling in Baskerville Old Face. It has been printed letterpress in
Great Britain by Balding & Mansell Ltd, of London & Wisbech,
on Basingwerk Parchment supplied by Grosvenor Chater Ltd,
and bound by Wm Brendon & Son Ltd, of Tiptree, Essex.

To Elizabeth David
with gratitude and affection

Introduction

Hugh Johnson, in his remarkable book *Wine*, says in his chapter on food and wine, 'What it all boils down to is that far too much is written and said about what goes with what, what goes before or after what, or what to do and what to avoid'. I heartily agree with him, and I hope and believe that we have avoided laying down the law to you in this book about eating and drinking.

We all like to think that we know a lot about cooking and wine, but what really matters is the pleasure and measure that good food and wine give to us in the company of those whom we love.

Here is how this book was born. About ten years ago I decided, with my friend and partner in Christopher's, Peter Noble, to send to our customers a leaflet about food and wine. Having undertaken to produce and edit it, I turned to my friend Elizabeth David for help. She agreed to provide the recipes, and we began with three small leaflets for Spring, Summer and Autumn. With encouragement from our customers we became more ambitious and the leaflet grew in size and scope into a monthly publication. After some three years, owing to the increased demands of her books and business interests, Elizabeth David 'retired'. But she continued to make contributions, and always gave me her invaluable critical advice.

I then gathered my material from friends, both amateur and professional, and enlarged my articles on wine to make them more topical and less commercial. At this time Yvonne Skargon created, for each month of the year, the wood-cut engravings which have been so much admired, and which form such an important part of the book.

The book is divided into twelve monthly chapters, selected from the hundreds of leaflets sent out to our customers. In many ways it is due to their enthusiasm that we have made this book, and I am very grateful for their encouragement. It does not set out to be a textbook on eating and drinking because there are, after all, many such books written by people more qualified than I.

I have tried to give to my own contributions on wine a more

personal, and less technical, flavour than is customary in the pronouncements of professional writers. They have already given so much admirable advice on the marriage of food and wine that it does not need repetition in a book of this type. We have included the price of wines, together with the date when they were quoted, purely as a matter of interest and to point out the frightening inflation that has taken place in the last ten years.

Lastly, I am indebted to so many people for their articles, help and advice, that I cannot possibly mention them all by name. Some of their names appear in this book; but to all of them I say, 'Accept my thoughts for thanks; I have no words.'

OLOF WIJK
94 Jermyn Street, SW1

January

Ice bears: boys slide.
GILBERT WHITE 1775

A right and a left

There are few things more enjoyable than to wake up on a Sunday morning, in the dead of winter, knowing that one has nothing to do except to arrive, on time, for luncheon at the home of friends who love good food and wine.

Little did I know, when I rang the bell of their house, that this was going to be my hour of triumph. Greetings over, I was given a glass of champagne and before I could take a sip my hostess, who is a musician of considerable talent, said to me, 'You have arrived exactly at the right time. You think you know something about music, tell us quickly who is singing this song and who composed it?' There was the voice proceeding from a record or the radio and there was the question. I took a large mouthful of champagne and gathered my wits about me; panic gripped me. 'Schwarzkopf! The song I don't know, but it must be Strauss,' I spluttered. I was right, and my friends were faintly impressed!

At lunch, with the roast lamb, my host filled my glass with red wine and said casually, 'Perhaps you would like to tell us the name and year of this wine and pull off the double!' Now I took my time (and if you hear these stories of people who frequently name, correctly, a wine by name and year, don't believe them!), and a chain of dim memories started to come back to me; colour, flavour, and a very special finesse and bouquet – this wine and I were old friends, but when and where? Schwarzkopf's voice was fresh in my mind, and if my ear had stored up in my brain the particular timbre of her voice, then perhaps my palate might have imprinted a memory of this wine which would come to my aid now. The wine was smooth, light in texture, and subtly penetrating in flavour and bouquet. It was the 'silver' of the flute, certainly not the 'rich brown' of the 'cello. Suddenly I sensed that the voice and the wine were linked together in the early 1950's and that I had heard the voice and drunk the wine at about the same time. Then I knew there was one wine which matched the quality of this voice at that time – Château Haut Brion 1944. Before I uttered the name I knew I was right.

A Right and Left with a vengeance! And to think I am a very bad shot and can't sing a note in tune; but my ear is quite good, and my palate is no worse, nor better, than most lovers of wine. It just amounts to memory and bags of luck! If Miss Schwarzkopf will forgive the term applied to her voice and artistry, I can pay no higher compliment to her and Château Haut Brion by saying that they are both *Premiers Crûs*.

FOOTNOTE   Later in the same week Tony Berry, famous wine merchant of St James's Street, generously produced at dinner in his home a bottle of Château Haut Brion 1923, because he remembered my enthusiasm for this vintage. Luckily for me I did not have to make a guess, but I wonder what Ladbroke's would have laid against the double of 1944 and 1923 Château Haut Brion? I still have the 1953 Vintage of Schwarzkopf and Strauss' *Four Last Songs*. Alas! It is no longer available; but listen to the 1966 Vintage on Columbia CX 5258 and you will understand what I mean by *Premier Crû*!

Taste and memory

But let me die, my love, yes, let me die;
With love and patience let your true love die;
Your grief and fury hurts my second life.
Yet let me kiss my lord before I die,
And let me die with kissing of my lord.

I will instruct my sorrows to be proud;
For grief is proud and makes his owner stoop.
To me and to the state of my great grief
Let Kings assemble; for my grief's so great
That no supporter but the huge firm earth
Can hold it up: here I and sorrows sit;
Here is my throne, bid Kings come bow to it.

Some fifty years ago I remember my step-father mentioning with admiration and affection the name of his friend Maurice Baring; but it was my loss that I never met him. However, I never forgot his name, and in 1936, the year I joined Christopher's, Heinemann published his book which, ever since, has been a constant and delightful companion. The book, as he says in the preface, is the literary baggage with which he had travelled throughout his life – two boxes labelled MEMORY and NOTES from which he made his Customs House declaration – and it is aptly named *Have You Anything to Declare?*. Of the two passages quoted above he writes, 'Before making up one's mind whether Shakespeare or Marlowe wrote Richard III, it is a good thing to taste a piece of undisputed Shakespeare, place it beside a piece of undisputed Marlowe, and compare the rhythm of both.' Maybe your palate will have no difficulty in solving the problem. But what delights me is Baring's use of the word 'taste' – what I would call a lesson in the art of poetry tasting!

Because we are constantly using our senses of sight and hearing, the 'sight-brain memory' and 'sound-brain memory' produce some remarkable instances of immediate recognition and identification, which often astonish us by their accuracy. Although it must be forty years since I saw Steve Donoghue ride a race horse, if an old newsreel was flashed on to my television set, I would back myself to pick him out instantly, by his inimitable style, from amongst a large field of jockeys. One only has to hear Peter O'Sullevan's or Michael Seth-Smith's reading of a horse-race to marvel at the accuracy of their 'sight-brain memory'.

But, as well as the all-important sense of sight, the tasting of wine brings in the senses of smell and taste – both of which we consciously exercise in daily life far less frequently than sight. It is here that I wish to strongly recommend to you a little book called *Wine Tasting*. Written by Michael Broadbent, Master of Wine, it tells you everything that I would have been proud to have written on this fascinating subject. It is a lucid lesson in the art of tasting wine. After reading it, I hope you may be encouraged to organize with your friends your own tastings at home.

Like the tasting of Marlowe and Shakespeare, the first rule in wine tasting, if you wish to gain maximum learning and enjoyment, is to taste 'blind', however simple the lesson in question; no sight of label, nor even of the shape of the bottle, must be allowed to bias your judgement. All the basic points to make a wine tasting successful are clearly set out in Michael Broadbent's book.

A January Dinner

Not all the junketing of Christmas and the New Year, together with that bountiful goodwill shown to some, if not all, men can anaesthetize us to the awful blows of Welfare State, delivered all too early in the New Year in the form of Income Tax, school bills, electricity blackouts, rising fuel costs and so on, to say nothing of the bills for the now-forgotten junketing, goodwill, etc. Let us see therefore if there is not some small crumb of compensation to be found in this remorseless month.

Economy must be our watch-word, but let us not be foolishly economical and deny ourselves all the pleasures of the table in an orgy of financial martyrdom. Thus we will start with a simple, easy-to-make, but very good terrine.

TERRINE

1 lb. liver (chicken, duck, pig, lamb, etc), ½ lb. seasoned pork sausage meat, 1 teaspoonful marjoram, 2 oz. butter, six rashers of streaky bacon, a few mushrooms, pepper, salt and garlic.

Use any kind of liver you like or a mixture of several. Put through a fine mincer. Melt the butter and mix with the liver. Add seasoning and the herbs (marjoram or what you will). Add some crushed garlic too. Take a shallow oval pie dish, line the bottom with the bacon, from which you have taken off all rind and bone, and cover with half of the liver mixture. Take the sausage meat, flour it well and roll out on a board. Cover with mushrooms, finely chopped, fold in half and roll out again. Fold and roll a second time and then shape to the contour of the dish, but about half an inch smaller all round. Lay it on top of the liver mixture in the dish and then cover with the remainder of the mixture. Cover with tin foil and stand in a baking dish with sufficient water to come two-thirds up the sides. Cook in a moderate oven, 300°F for 1¾ hours. When cooked pour off excess fat, place a suitable plate or other flat surface on top, weight it and leave to get quite cold. The contents, which will have shrunk during the cooking process, will then have spread out again to reach the sides of the dish and will be quite solid. If the terrine is to be kept it should be covered with melted lard to exclude all air.

Covered once again with tin-foil it will last for months. If required for immediate use the top may be decorated according to inclination and energy and, in any event covered with a little nicely seasoned aspic jelly.

BEEF STEW

Go to your butcher and buy a pound of the cheapest beef he can find. If you have any silly ideas about loss of face you can always tell him that you are going to give your dog a treat. Cut this meat (box-cut, shin, chuck, or whatever it may be) into neat, matchbox-size pieces. Neatness at this stage is important as it will give a professional look to the finished dish. Fry these pieces in a little fat until browned on all sides and then put them into a saucepan. Cut up two medium onions and fry in the same pan until they turn golden, then add four tomatoes, cut in quarters, a few black or green olives, halved and stoned, a diced carrot and a few slices of aubergine if such is available. Allow all to fry together for a few moments. Add $\frac{1}{2}$ teaspoonful thyme or mixed herbs, pepper and salt, and two cloves of garlic, cut up into tiny pieces. Stir in two glasses of red wine and then add to the meat in the saucepan. Add a little more wine if necessary, just enough to cover the contents of the pan. Put a piece of greaseproof paper over the saucepan and then ram the lid down as tight as you can. Stew very, very gently for at least four hours. When you ultimately lift the lid, the glorious aroma of this superb stew will alter your whole view of life, even before you have discovered its even more glorious taste!

BANANA CREOLE

Put a generous spoonful of orange marmalade in the bottom of an oven-proof dish. Lay peeled bananas flat on the bottom and then sprinkle with brown sugar, a few currants and sultanas and a little chopped mixed peel. Pour over a glass of rum and bake in a slow oven for about forty-five minutes to an hour. Garnish with whipped cream and serve piping hot.

LESLIE HOARE

More Food for January

ESCALOPES DE VEAU EN PAPILLOTES

For four people buy four escalopes of veal each weighing 3–4 oz.; other ingredients are ½ lb. of mushrooms, four slices of cooked ham cut fairly thin and as much as possible the same shape as the escalopes, 1 medium-sized onion, 2 oz. of butter, a bunch of parsley and seasonings including lemon juice. You also need four sheets of good quality greaseproof paper.

Melt 1 oz. of the butter in a thick frying pan. In this lightly brown on both sides the escalopes, already seasoned with salt and lemon juice. Keep them aside while you cook the finely chopped onion in the same butter. Don't let the onion brown; it must be thoroughly softened, but still yellow and translucent.

Now add another ½ oz. of butter, and the mushrooms. These should be washed (not peeled), dried with a soft cloth, and finely chopped. While they are in the pan sprinkle them with salt and freshly milled pepper. When their juice runs, stir in 2 tablespoonfuls of chopped parsley.

To prepare the papillotes or paper cases fold the sheets of greaseproof paper, each measuring about 20 inches × 10 inches, in two. Cut these 10 inch squares into a heart shape, the point at the open end.

Butter one half of each paper; and on the butter lay the escalope; on top put the slice of ham, and spread this with a portion of the mushroom mixture. Fold up the paper, and twist the edges securely together.

All these preparations can be made in advance. When the time comes to cook the papillotes, put them on a flat dish near the top of a moderately hot oven, gas No.4, 350°F, and leave them for about twenty minutes.

Serve them as they are, so that each guest unwraps his own. You will need finger bowls, and a dish to take the bits of paper. You will not need any extra vegetable. The veal and the delicious mushroom and onion should be savoured on their own.

ELIZABETH DAVID

CIVET DE LIÈVRE LANDAIS

Have the hare cut into the usual pieces. Brown them slightly in goose or pork fat. In an earthenware casserole brown twelve shallots chopped fine, two or three cloves of garlic, and ½ lb. of bacon or gammon cut in dice (in the Landes they use *Jambon de Bayonne*). Add a glass of red wine, let it reduce a little, add two glasses of stock or water and a tablespoonful of thick tomato purée (or six ripe tomatoes previously grilled and skinned) and an ounce of dried cèpes. Put in the pieces of hare, cover the casserole and cook very slowly for two to three hours, until the hare is quite tender.

The sauce should by this time be sufficiently reduced to need no further thickening, but if it is too thin, pour if off into a wide pan, keeping the hare hot in the casserole, and reduce it very quickly for a few minutes.

Notes

The 'hare lip' is much more developed in an old hare than a young one.

Hare should always be over- rather than undercooked.

The long bone in the back leg of a hare, if suitably drilled at either end, the marrow blown out, and then boiled, makes a practical cigarette holder, which colours with much the richness of meerschaum.

'Take your hare when it is cased. . .' HANNAH GLASSE, *Art of Cookery*. Usually misquoted as 'First catch your hare.'

'To make a ragout, first catch your hare.' (Pour faire un civet, prenez un lièvre.) LA VARENNE, *Le Cusinier Français*, p. 40. Quoted by Metternich from Marchioness of Londonderry, *Narrative of a Visit to the Courts of Vienna*. In a cook book published in 1947, attributed to Dr Hill. See *Notes and Queries*, 10 Sept., 1859, p. 206.

ELIZABETH DAVID

ROAST MILK-FED LAMB

A leg is the best joint for this dish – or two if they are very small. You can have it boned or not, as you wish. Heat some olive oil in a baking-tin in a very hot oven. Pour some more oil over the joint and rub in some finely chopped garlic. Make a bed of rosemary in the baking-tin and put in the joint. Cook for ten minutes, then turn the oven down. Turn the joint frequently and baste with oil. Season with salt, pepper and nutmeg towards the end of the cooking. A small joint takes about ¾ hour – it should be brown outside and just pink within.

Some like a green vegetable so I suggest sprouts and, for those who are bored with them, a purée of celeriac. You should be able to get Canary Island potatoes, though they are not very interesting: cook them with mint and salt, drain, toss them in butter with a squeeze of lemon-juice.

ROBIN MCDOUALL

CHESTNUTS WITH KIRSCH

Shelled and skinned chestnuts are simmered gently in water and with a little sugar and a vanilla pod until they are quite tender, but the greatest care must be taken to see that they do not break up. Leave them to cook in their syrup, then put half a dozen or so into a large wine glass for each person, with a very little of the syrup. Pour a couple of tablespoonfuls of Alsatian or Swiss Kirsch into each. The Kirsch that you do not use for the Chestnuts will be invaluable for fruit salads.

Alternatively, serve the French tinned chestnuts in syrup in the same fashion. Either way this dessert is for the very rich or the very extravagant.

ELIZABETH DAVID

B

POIRES ROUGES

Four dessert pears, 4 oz. sugar, 1 teaspoonful arrowroot, 1½ gills port or red wine, ½ teaspoonful cinnamon, strip lemon peel, 1 tablespoonful redcurrant jelly or jam, ¼ pint whipped cream, flaked browned almonds.

Dissolve sugar in wine with lemon peel and cinnamon. Peel pears, cut them lengthwise and core. Place in saucepan with wine, adding enough water to barely cover. Simmer gently, turning occasionally for forty minutes or until tender. Remove from syrup and arrange, cut side uppermost, on a flat dish. Slake arrowroot with a little water in a cup until smooth. Pour some of the hot syrup on this, stirring. Return this to the saucepan of syrup and add jam. Stir until it boils. Simmer two minutes. Strain over pears. Chill well. Pipe large rosettes of whipped cream into the hollow of each pear half. Scatter over the browned flaked almonds.

PRUDENCE LEITH

RHUBARB FOOL

It is hard to improve on stewed rhubarb when it is fresh and young (cooked in the oven with a little water and some granulated sugar) but it is hardly a dinner-party dish; so cook more than you need and use the rest for a fool. Put it through a mill. Sweeten. Make some custard (with eggs and milk, not out of a packet). Mix equal quantities of custard and cream with the rhubarb purée. Serve in a glass bowl with a sauceboat of whipped cream and sponge fingers handed separately.

ROBIN MCDOUALL

Wine and Food Notes for January

So much has been said, written and pontificated on the various marriages between wine and food, let alone the divorces!, that I have no intention of turning this book into a marriage guidance bureau on the harmonious relationship between wine and food. All I intend to do is to repeat some of the notes and hints I have made, over the years, in my wine and food leaflets in the hope that they will give you some ideas which will be useful.

In his book *Wines* (Penguin, 6s.) Allan Sichel gives you some rules and conventions governing the selection of wines to accompany food. They are adaptable, simple and logical and I strongly recommend you to read chapter 5 of this excellent book. Meanwhile, when all is said and done, each one of us has tastes which vary widely, and we all have the right to our own opinion in all matters of taste. Variety being the spice of life may be a cliché, but provided that variety is not carried to extremes, and I can think of several, then it should be possible to experiment within certain limits with your choice of wines and food and provoke discussion and argument between you and your friends.

As an example, in January 1964 I wrote: 'Most white wines taste metallic with smoked salmon. The exception? Sauternes or Barsac, served well chilled. We recommend Ch. Coutet, Barsac, 1950, 20s the bottle.' (I shudder to think of the price today.) This suggestion and departure from dry white wine with smoked salmon provoked sarcastic comment from a well known wine writer and friend of mine who has since publicly reversed his criticism and given his blessing to this particular marriage.

January is a month which invariably brings us cold and wet weather, so choose young red wines with plenty of body, especially with such dishes as the Beef Stew and Casserole of Hare. Young wines benefit from being decanted several hours before the meal and left to breathe and slowly acquire room temperature; it is well worth your trouble.

With the dish of Veal I recommend an Alsatian wine such as Pinot Blanc or Traminer; be careful not to overchill your white wine in winter.

This is the month to experiment with the richer Oloroso sherries and Madeiras, such as Bual and Malmsey. They fit in with soups, and at the end of a meal with puddings, fruit, or the strong flavoured cheeses.

Next time you drink a glass of Ruby Port eat a Cox's Orange Pippin. You will be delighted with the harmony of flavours.

February

O, thought I! what a beautiful thing God has made winter to be, by
stripping the trees, and letting us see their shapes and forms. What a
freedom does it seem to give to the storms!

DOROTHY WORDSWORTH 1802

In concert

And, if you must know, life is often ashes. For some, it's a wonderful thing with desperate moments. For others it's a desperate thing with wonderful moments.

From *The Family Man*, a novel by JOHN GALE.

'I have never met anyone as happy as I am.' Thus spoke Artur Rubinstein in December 1968, in the eighty-fourth year of his full and hard-working life; and even if my message does not reach you until February, my wish for you all is a full measure of happiness, good health and peace in 1969.

It was in 1967 that Rubinstein undertook the prodigious task of playing consecutively, at one sitting, the 3rd, 4th and 5th piano concertos of Beethoven. As I sat and listened in rapture and wonder at his virtuosity and the genius of the composer, I realized that I had a unique opportunity to decide, once and for all, which concerto was my favourite. As I suspected, the 4th proved to be the winner. After the concert I fell to wondering, supposing I was offered a feast of three wines comparable in quality to these concertos, which would I choose, and how would I allocate them? Red wines they surely must be; and from one district. The Médoc? Yes! Ch. Margaux (the Queen) to the 3rd, Ch. Lafite (the King) to the 4th, Ch. Latour (the Emperor) to the 5th.

Fantasy, you might say, and you would be right, because I have never been lucky enough to taste these three wines at one meal. Certainly I would not be sure of recognizing my favourite of the three at the first sip, whereas the 4th piano concerto, to me, is unmistakable, because Beethoven, ignoring precedent, opens on the piano with a miraculous and quiet five bar phrase, which is completed by the orchestra, and of which I never tire.

Where is all this leading to? Well, just before this memorable concert, Rubinstein was interviewed on Jack de Manio's programme 'Today'. Inevitably he was asked, 'Which is your favourite piece of Chopin?' To this he wisely replied, 'Ah! that is a luxury reserved for amateurs. My favourite piece of Chopin is the one I am playing at the time.' And so, I believe, it is with wine. Whether one be amateur or professional, it is the wine you are drinking at the time which should be your favourite.

Since we cannot all afford the great trio from the Médoc, there is fortunately a more varied Triple Concerto from the Rhône. However, like Beethoven's Concerto for Piano, Violin and 'Cello, there is always the practical difficulty of co-ordinating three top-notch soloists. But I believe we have succeeded in doing this below.

LE CHEVALIER DE STERIMBERG Blanc, 1966	26/–
COTE ROTIE, 1959	31/6
HERMITAGE LA CHAPELLE, 1957	31/6

All bottled at the domaine by Paul Jaboulet.

February 1969

André Louis Simon

BORN 28TH FEBRUARY 1877

It seems almost audacious for me, a mere stripling in his sixty-first year, to pay tribute to André Simon on his ninetieth birthday, when there are so many others more fitted for the task. Nevertheless, I do possess three curious links with this Grand Old Man of Letters and Gastronomy.

In 1897 André Simon wished to send some wine to his fiancée in England. He chanced to see an advertisement in *The Times Weekly* inserted by a firm called Christopher's of Pall Mall, resulting in an order which I like to believe was the first to be received by any London wine merchant from the man who was on the threshold of seventy years' work in the cause of good food and wine.

In 1919, when, after my father's death, my mother married Reggie Barnes, cavalry officer, General, and old friend of Winston Churchill, it was from him I first heard the name of Pommery, the champagne which André Simon had made famous since he set up his business in 1902, at No. 24 Mark Lane as Madame Pommery's London Agent. The link was Pommery champagne in the shape of Percy Thellusson, a staff officer at my stepfather's Divisional H.Q. in France and André Simon's partner – my stepfather never forgot his luck!

Thirdly, on the 28th February my mother will be the guest o

her old friend Mrs Starr at The Wine & Food Society's banquet in honour of André Simon's ninetieth birthday. Mrs Starr is ninety-one and the oldest living member of the Society; so on that day three people will sit down whose combined ages date back to John Dryden in the reign of William and Mary!

But the real link, forged in his immortal books, lectures and propaganda, is the debt that the whole Wine Trade owes to André Simon, its greatest disciple. As a founder of the Wine Trade Club in 1908 he was, in every sense of the word, a pioneer in the education of the young men of our Trade, and, later through the Wine and Food Society, of the public. The Club provided facilities for these young men to attend tastings, lectures, technical education and for the formation of a library of books, all of which was completely unheard of in those days, and even frowned on by the older members of the Wine Trade as new-fangled ideas.

The year before I was born, his first book, *The History of the Champagne Trade in England*, was printed and sold for 5s. od. for the benefit of the Wine & Spirit Trade's Benevolent Society. The subsequent titles of his immense bibliography are the jewels in the crown of wine and food. Today, in an age when cookery books and wine books are two a penny (and so much the better!) we must never forget his implacable struggle in the cause of quality, of both wine and food, in this country of his adoption.

As a man I would call him gentle, sincere and extremely good humoured, warm hearted and affectionate. Above all I admire his complete lack of affectation and his ability to get the younger generation to talk freely, and to listen to what they have to say. The emphasis of all his works has been on quality with simplicity. The clarity of his mind at the age of ninety is extraordinary, and it may well be that his greatest monument will be his last book, *A Gazetteer of Wine*, on which his is now working. The wish of Christopher's is that he may live for many more years to enjoy the good food and wine of which he is the greatest living advocate.

February 1967

One man's meat . . .

A man must serve his time to every trade save censure – critics all are ready made. GEORGE GORDON, LORD BYRON, 1788–1824

I am happy to report an excellent vintage of 'Figaro' this year. GUARDIAN

It is rarely that one encounters a 'Figaro' so unsatisfactory on every level as the Glyndebourne performance. FINANCIAL TIMES

'Figaro', 1964 Vintage, appears to have made very different impressions on the 'palates' of these two critics! As a matter of personal 'taste' I enjoy 'Non Vintage' Mozart, and am not over-particular whether it is the Domaine bottling of Glyndebourne or Covent Garden in 1962 or 1964, providing it is genuine 'Produce of Mozart' of sound quality. However, I do recognize that critics of music, and wine, fulfil a purpose in life and I am prepared to listen to their 'tasting' of individual vintages of 'Figaro', which may have escaped my untutored 'palate' or ear.

Music and wine (and, for that matter, cricket) lend themselves to snobbery, and we are well aware of this when we presume to tell you what wines you should buy and enjoy. Individual palates, like critics, will differ widely about the qualities of a particular wine, but we do protest against the serving of Ch. d'Yquem 1955 with oysters at a recent Paris banquet, let alone the correspondent's description of this imcomparable Sauternes as 'a sweet White Bordeaux'!

All this leads me to tell you that, if the 1964 Vintage of 'Figaro' may have been uneven in Glyndebourne, in Chablis they made some superb wine in 1964. Unlike genuine Mozart (which is always *appellation contrôlée*.) Chablis has many spurious imitators and labels. As a companion to shellfish (*pace* Ch. d'Yquem 1955!) genuine Chablis has few equals. We invite your criticism of our Chablis Quartet, Opus 1964.

CHABLIS PREMIER CRU, LA FOURCHAUME, 1964	18/6
CHABLIS PREMIER CRU, VAILLONS, 1964	26/–
CHABLIS PREMIER CRU, VAULORENT, 1964	26/–
CHABLIS GRAND CRU, LES PREUSES, 1964	29/6

February 1966

Australia

Fan – *used from about 1900 as an abbreviation of 'fanatic' (q.v.), an ardent admirer or devotee. Admiring letters written to the object of such devotion are known as 'fan mail'.*

BREWER'S DICTIONARY OF PHRASE AND FABLE

For some years now I must confess to being an inveterate writer of fan mail to people I have never met, nor am ever likely to meet, but who have enriched my life by their words or deeds.

All fans will understand me when I say that the first thing one must learn, in the early days of fanaticism, is never to count on or expect answers to fan mail; if this priciple is not accepted, one is doomed to some bitter disappointments. After all, if you love and admire your friends, you don't expect them to thank you; and the objects of my fan mail are my friends even if I never expect to meet them or hear from them.

When still a schoolboy, Australia, to me, was a very large island coloured pink on the map, many weeks and many thousands of miles away, famous for its wool, cricket, tennis players, singers and tough fighting men. It was not until 1941 that I first rubbed shoulders with Australians and grew to love them, and acquired a steadfast ambition to visit their country before I die.

Meanwhile I am content and proud to have several Australian friends, and to listen to them talk of their homeland. They are a happy and unspoilt people, and make me realize and be thankful for the deep bonds which exist between our two countries.

Imagine, therefore, my pleasure to receive, in answer to one of my fan letters, these words from their greatest living statesman:

'Whatever we may say, we all like a word of encouragement, and I am most grateful for yours.' In these difficult days, for both Britain and the Commonwealth, we all need to receive and give encouragement to each other. Australian wines deserve encouragement for their intrinsic quality, and recently I have tasted two red wines which are worthy examples of their viticulture, and which, despite devaluation, are excellent value for money. Please taste them – without condescension – because they compare favourably with wines from Europe at similar prices.

ORION DRY, light red wine   12/−
ORION RICH, full red wine   12/−

February 1968

The Food for February

GASTROENTERWRITERS

It was, I believe, Mr Francis Hope of the *New Statesman* who, some fifteen months ago, rounded up a half dozen over-solemn, overweight, overpriced and under-instructive volumes of gastronomic literature, wrote a deflating review of the whole batch, and dubbed their authors gastronauts. The invention was a good one, although perhaps gastroenterwriters would be even more appropriate.

'I am the man', one of our brave gastroenterwriters, then, is reported as declaring, 'I am the man who brought French cuisine to the British'. In the year AD 1965 that seems a pretty serious claim. Considering it soberly, it is difficult not to wonder whatever became of 1066 and the nine centuries during which French cooking has taken root, grown, and flourished in English kitchens.

The gentleman does, however, raise a point. Who are, who were, the writers responsible for the propagation of the gospel of French cooking in these islands? To me it would seem that English and French traditions of cookery are too inextricably interwoven to allow of arbitrary division into two separate streams. To say that this cookery writer wrote only of French cookery, that one exclusively of English cookery, is to attempt to divide the indivisible. Every author who writes about cookery in the English language and for English readers is, by implication, writing about English cookery. If he is not, then he might as well write his book in Chinese or Armenian. At the same time, however staunchly British and John Bull-ish he might be, he will find it a practical impossibility to avoid altogether any reference to French cooking and French methods, even if it is only for the sake of comparison, and to discover in what fashion a nine-hundred-year-old tradition has developed.

Toward appreciation of these points, increased familiarity with our own cookery history and its literature, so astonishingly rich, varied, and illuminating, would help.

To take just one example out of scores, there is the case of William Verral, whose little book *The Cook's Paradise* was published in 1759. No man could have been more English by birth, breeding, occupation, outlook. To be precise, Verral was a Sussex inn-keeper, master of the White Hart at Lewes. At this inn, still flourishing, where Verral's father before him had presided, the young Verral was apprenticed to St Clouet, a French chef in the service of Thomas Pelham Hollis, Duke of Newcastle, a member of the great Sussex landowning family of Pelham, and for thirty years George the Second's notoriously incompetent Minister of State.

Most of William Verral's recipes, were, so he tells us, learned from St Clouet, and indeed from Verral's phonetic French spelling (nantiles for lentilles, glass for glacé, pauvrade for poivrade) it is easy to deduce that they were noted down from direct dictation, and subsequently rendered into Verral's own breezy, colloquial English. From *The Cook's Paradise*, however allegedly French the recipes, emerges a vivid little picture of what we should now consider honest, old-fashioned, English country cooking as practised in the chief coaching inn of an important county town. Here, for example, is Verral's version of macaroni cheese, a dish which, clearly, came to us from French rather than from Italian kitchens, for Verral calls macaroni macarons or macaroons, and includes two recipes for them among his sweet dishes and entremets, or what we should now call savouries.

WILLIAM VERRAL'S MACARONI WITH PARMESAN CHEESE

'These are to be had at any confectioner's in London and the newer they are the better – this is not what we call macaroons of the sweet biscuit sort, but a foreign paste, the same as vermicelly, but made very large in comparison to that – For this you must boil them in water first, with a little salt, pour on them a ladle of

28

cullis,[1] a morsel of green onion and parsley minced fine, pepper, salt and nutmeg; stew all a few minutes, and pour into a dish with a rim, squeeze a lemon or orange, and cover it over pretty thick with Parmesan cheese grated very fine, bake it of a fine colour, about a quarter of an hour, and serve it up hot.

'The French serve to their tables a great many dishes with this sort of cheese, and in the same manner, only sometimes with a savoury white sauce, such as scallops, oysters, and many of the things you have among these entremets'.

ELIZABETH DAVID

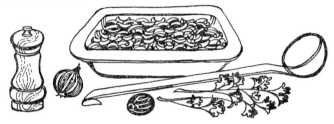

A February Menu

Lenten menus pose several problems: some people – and this may include host or hostess – do not really like an all fish meal, and shellfish are an unwise choice unless the ability of all guests to eat them is known in advance. But a too 'eggy' dish is not the best partner for fine wines; and although a cheese or spinach soufflé superbly done, can form a main course at all but the most formal of dinners these days, the exactness of the timing can be difficult for the single handed cook-host. This menu attempts to smooth out all difficulties for a small dinner or after-theatre supper party, and you could serve either a white or red wine. The main course will not be a disaster if it has to wait five minutes.

Smoked fish are always a popular first course and this canapé-cum-open-sandwich is an attractive 'starter', especially if it is thought that a whole plate of smoked salmon, eel, or trout may be too much.

[1] Coulis or cullis was the basic brown sauce of highly concentrated meat stock thickened with flour and butter, which was all-important in eighteenth-century cookery.

SMOKED SALMON AND CREAMED CHEESE

Beat up some cream cheese, of the Chambourcy or similar type with some double cream, until it is fluffy and only just firm. Add chopped chives or finely chopped gherkins and spread it thickly on slices of pumpernickel. On the top of each slice, pile minced smoked salmon, sprinkle with a little black pepper and lemon juice. The mincing not only gives the smoked salmon a lightness and attractive appearance, but makes it go twice as far.

A main course that can be served or offered from just one dish enables everyone to get helpings while they are hot, including the host. Sweetcorn today is associated with the United States, and Maryland in particular. But the inhabitants of Franche Comté claim that it was settlers from this part of France who took the taste for maize across the Atlantic. It is also one of the few regions of France where sweetcorn is considered delicious fare and not merely cattle food!

MAIS EN SOUFFLÉ

For six persons: Drain a large tin of whole kernel corn and to it add a teaspoonful of paprika, a generous sprinkle of rock salt and a dessertspoonful of melted butter. Beat together four large or five standard eggs, ½ pint of milk and 4 oz. of grated cheese (half Parmesan and half Gruyère or Emmenthal is a good combination) then add this to the corn. Butter a soufflé or baking dish and put in half the mixture, then a layer of toasted breadcrumbs, then the rest of the mixture and top with another layer of crumbs and a few chips of butter. Bake in a moderate oven for thirty to forty minutes, when the top should be lightly brown and crisp. Serve as soon as possible.

A pleasant accompaniment is a salad of chicory, dressed lightly with oil and vinegar, and topped with a few coarsely crushed walnuts.

Pancakes, which seem to have been indulged in on Shrove Tuesday from the earliest times as a last fling before the Lenten fast, are suspiciously described by the Water Poet, in 1620: 'There is a thing call'd wheaten floure, which the cookes do mingle with water, eggs, spice and other tragicall, magicall enchantments, and then they put it by little and little into a frying pan of boiling suet, where it makes a confused dismall hissing, until at last by the skill of the Cooke it is transformed into the form of a Flip-Jack, call'd Pancake, which ominous incantation the ignorant people do devoure very greedilie'.

But those who do not want to cook the last course of the meal may prefer a refreshing orange salad, which can also be used as a pancake filling if desired.

SPANISH ORANGE SALAD

For each guest, take a medium-sized orange, remove the skin and all the pith and then slice the fruit across, taking out any pips. Arrange the circles of orange in a flat dish, sprinkle them lightly with cinnamon and, for each whole fruit, allow a dessertspoonful of Kirsch, Izarra or Cointreau. Chill well before serving.

PAMELA VANDYKE PRICE

More Food for February

KIDNEY SAUTÉ

A veal kidney is enough for four people. Trim off the skin and nerve and then cook the kidney lightly in a little butter. At the same time shred four rashers of streaky bacon and cook in butter until crisp. Stir in a heaped dessertspoonful of flour and add ½ pint water with a chicken bouillon cube in it, a dessertspoonful of tomato purée, a teaspoonful of French mustard, a couple of sliced mushrooms and a glass of Sherry. Stir well, season to taste and allow to simmer for a few moments. Take the kidney and cut it in slices; then add it, and the juice that may run out when slicing, to the sauce. Simmer very, very gently for fifteen minutes. This simple, inexpensive dish is really superb.

LESLIE HOARE

GOUGÈRE

This sophisticated little French savoury is usually made by piping cheese-flavoured choux pastry in rings on to a baking sheet. But it can be turned into a delightful first course by filling with a savoury mixture. With a little imagination one can use up all sorts of left-over bits and pieces, and I suggest the following recipe.

Make the choux pastry by boiling ¼ pint of water with 2 oz. butter and then, away from the heat, stir in 3 oz. plain flour until the mixture is quite smooth. When cool, stir in two beaten eggs, a little at a time, and then 2 oz. grated cheese. Pipe or spoon this mixture into little individual dishes, keeping it to the sides so that there is a clear space in the middle.

Chop a small onion and cook slowly in a little butter. When soft, add a dessertspoonful of flour and 2 pints of milk. Stir until think and smooth and then add about ½ lb. flaked cooked smoked haddock and a dessertspoonful of chopped parsley. Put this mixture into the middle of your gougère and leave in the refrigerator until required. At the last minute sprinkle with grated cheese and bake in a hot oven for fifteen to twenty minutes. The choux pastry will rise considerably to form a kind of dome, leaving the filling, as it were, *en surprise*.

LESLIE HOARE

CREAM OF CAULIFLOWER SOUP

I share with Elizabeth David a dislike for cauliflower cooked in its more ordinary and soggy ways; but I love this delicate creamy soup.

'For six people you need two medium-sized cauliflowers, 1¾ pints of bouillon, a glass of milk, 4 oz. butter, four yolks of egg, salt, but no pepper. Take off the outside leaves, separate into branches, wash it, and cook in very lightly salted water. When absolutely soft, drain it, pound it to a purée, and pass through a fine sieve, or pass through a liquidizer.

'Add this pureé to the bouillon and bring it to the boil very gradually over a low fire. Let it simmer for fifteen minutes. Draw off to the side of the stove and add a glass (about ¼ pint) of milk. Taste for too much or too little salt; if too much, add a little more milk. Add the butter, stirring as it melts. To finish, beat the yolks with half a glass of water, add them to the soup, heating gently but without letting it boil, so that the yolks thicken the soup into a cream.'

GALETTE DE POMMES DE TERRE

February is generally a cold and cheerless month. Even though spring is just round the corner, I am tired long before now of potatoes boiled, mashed, roast or baked. So here is my favourite way of cooking them, as Elizabeth David taught me.

'Peel about 1½ lb. of potatoes and slice them very thinly and evenly. Wash them in plenty of cold water. In a *thick* frying pan heat a tablespoonful of butter and one of oil (the mixture of butter and oil gives a good flavour, and the oil prevents the butter from burning). Put the potatoes into the pan and spread them evenly; season with nutmeg, salt and ground black pepper; turn the heat down as soon as they start to cook, cover the pan and leave them to cook gently for fifteen minutes; by this time the under surface will be browned and the potatoes coagulated in such a way as to make a pancake; turn the galette over and leave the other side to brown for three or four minutes'.

A 'mandoline', incidentally, is indispensable for slicing potatoes thinly, and can be bought at Elizabeth David's shop in Bourne Street, SW1.

PORK CHOPS BAKED WITH POTATOES

A simple and delicious dish for hungry people on a cold February day. four pork chops, 1½ lb. potatoes, a small glass of white wine or cider, one onion, two or three cloves of garlic, a few juniper berries, parsley, 4 oz. ham or bacon. Peel the potatoes and slice them evenly and very thinly. Arrange half of them, together with half the sliced onion, in an earthenware casserole.

Near the bone of each pork chop put a small piece of garlic and a couple of juniper berries. Brown them on each side in a little pork dripping. Put them on top of the potatoes, cover them with the remaining half of the potatoes and onion; season with salt and pepper. Cover with the bacon or ham in slices. Pour over the wine or cider. Put two or three layers of paper over the pot, then the lid. Cook in a very slow oven for about three hours. Before serving pour off some of the abundant fat and garnish with parsley.

ELIZABETH DAVID

PAVLOVA CAKES

For four people: four egg whites, 1 large teaspoonful vinegar, 8 oz. granulated sugar, ¼ pint cream whipped, passion fruit. First heat the oven to 475°F, gas No. 8. Whip the egg whites and vinegar to a stiff froth. Gradually add the sugar, always beating well. Line two 7-inch flan tins with moist brown paper and divide the mixture into these. Place in the top of the oven and immediately reduce the heat to 250°F, gas No. ½. Leave for one hour twenty minutes. Lift out the cakes by the brown paper, remove the paper and leave the cakes to cool upside down. Fill the recess in each cake with the whipped cream and cover with passion fruit.

You can buy tinned passion fruit from Robert Jackson of 172 Piccadilly – otherwise use fresh fruit salad, or other fruits in season.

At Christmas I was given a copy of *Celebrity Cooking*, edited by Renée Hellman, and originally published by Paul Hamlyn. It contains the favourite dishes of famous people from all walks of life and all parts of the world. A royalty from the sales of this book went to the Imperial Cancer Research Fund – which alone made it worth buying – and I guarantee you will find it fascinating and instructive reading. As I have been talking about Australia and am a great fan of Joan Sutherland, I have reproduced, above, her own particular recipe from *Celebrity Cooking*.

Wine hints and suggestions

I know of no better 'Valentine' than a bottle of champagne, particularly if you are there to share it with the recipient! If it is a bottle of Louis Roederer Cristal, I know of no better champagne.

As an aperitif, make a change this month from your usual Sherry and drink Sercial, the driest of the Madeiras. It will also make a challenging partner to Cream of Cauliflower soup.

Talking of aperitifs, do try out some of the more unusual Vermouths. Most of the Italian Vermouths come from around Turin, where is made a pungent bitter-sweet wine called Punt e Mes. Drink it, well chilled, with a twist of lemon peel. I admit that women like it better than men.

The Baked Pork Chops demand a crisp, clean and dry white wine with a certain amount of acidity to offset the fattiness of this dish. I suggest a young Pouilly Fuissé, or the white wine from Carcassonne called Limoux Marée. Serve lightly chilled.

To provoke discussion, and a 'country of origin' quiz, you might like to drink an Australian red wine with the Kidney Sauté. Decant the wine so that it may remain anonymous, and wait for your friends' comments and guess work. Most enterprising wine merchants stock the better quality Australian wines.

In February 1969 I wrote: 'What of 1969? Certainly it is the year of that excellent Scotch Whisky VAT 69! Meanwhile, 1969 has other connotations, if you read it upside down it becomes 6961 which I hope presages as good a vintage in 1969 as the superb wines of 1961. And just to emphasize the significance of 1961, turn it over and it will still read 1961!' So, since I am an ardent fan of the clarets of that year, I strongly advise you to pick them up when and wherever you can. The lesser wines, (if there are such things in this wonderful year), are good for drinking now. But there is no hurry; they will be your favourites for many years. The greater wines you must treasure patiently for the magnificent pleasure in store for you.

Mulled wine is always a success at winter parties and is simple to prepare. From each bottle you will get five to six large glasses. Simmer, but do not boil, the wine in an enamel saucepan with, (for every bottle), two cloves, a pinch of nutmeg, a slice of lemon and a heaped teaspoonful of sugar. You should taste regularly whilst preparing the brew, in order to get a good balance of sugar and cloves. A full bodied Spanish Rioja is suitable for a mulled cup.

March

After breakfast I walked with Jane and Helen Dew for a charming walk. We loitered through some lovely woods and dingles starred thick with primroses, and across a rushing brook upon the stepping stones. There was a sweet stirring of new life among the woods and a dawn of green upon the larches and hawthorns.

FRANCIS KILVERT 1874

When I demanded of my friend what viands he preferred,
He quoth: 'A large cold bottle, and a small hot bird.'
EUGENE FIELD, 1850–95

Until a few days ago I had not the faintest idea of what to write about for the month of March, and the nearer the deadline for submitting my copy, the more blank my mind seemed to become.

However, it was our English climate that finally came to my rescue, one winter's morning last week, when the thermometer in my bedroom barely registered 40°F! The usual mental tussle took place – whether or not I would take my morning swim. (No! Not in the Serpentine!) Half an hour later I was striding out on the two-mile walk, through a biting wind, to my swimming pool, which I reached with streaming eyes, blue nose and numb hands. Imagine my state of mind when, just as I was ready to plunge in, one of the 'regulars' shouted 'Watch out! You're in for a shock!' 'Heavens alive', I said to myself, 'I suppose the heating has broken down.'

In I went, amid peals of laughter, to find myself in a hot bath. Yes! the heating had gone wrong, upwards, to 83°F! At the end of my eight lengths I felt lethargic, exhausted and unrefreshed. Thank goodness, the next day the temperature was back to its normal 73°F.

To me, and to everyone who wants to drink wine at its best, the temperature of my wine is just as important to my full enjoyment as the temperature of my morning swim.

White Wines

Like my morning swim, I want my white wines to be refreshing, but not so cold that my palate is numbed and both bouquet and flavour are frozen. They should be chilled enough to curb their initial sweetness, which will then develop with their individual flavours in the warmth of your mouth. As a basic rule, chill a sweet wine a little more than a dry wine. Very fine quality wines with bottle age, particularly Burgundies, Sauternes and Hocks, should be drunk lightly chilled or at cellar temperature because the bouquet and flavour are all important. This also applies to very dry wines such as a fine quality Pouilly Blanc Fumé.

Red Wines

So that they may mature slowly from youth to age, red wines are kept in cool cellars. To drink them, they must be brought to a warmer temperature, so that the ethers produced in the process of maturing, and imprisoned in the bottle, can be released for your enjoyment. This warming process must be gradual. Ideally you should leave your bottle in room temperature for twenty-four hours. But whatever method you use, do not stand the bottle in front of a coal fire or an electric radiator, where one side becomes over-heated. Put it where it can be surrounded by warm air from a convector heater or a hot water radiator, or in some special place in the kitchen. If a red wine is overheated, the bouquet and flavour will have disappeared before it reaches your mouth. It is better to underdo the operation, because the warmth of your hands round the bowl of the glass can quickly bring the wine to the right temperature.

Malt Whisky

'The Government seems to regard Whisky as a dollar earner abroad and an evil at home.'

SIR ROBERT BRUCE LOCKHART. *Scotch*

'I wish I'd never started drinking Malt Whisky!' so writes one of my friends on re-ordering yet again one of our Malt Whiskies after a lifetime of drinking a brand of Blended Whisky. No higher compliment could be paid to the skill and traditions of the Malt Distilleries.

I do not expect to convert all my readers so easily to the delights of Malt Whisky, but I do hope that you will be tempted to taste some of them.

The original Whisky was made from malted barley dried over a peat fire, mashed with natural hill or spring water, and distilled in a simple pot still. There are about a hundred distilleries in Scotland today that still adhere meticulously to the ancient method of production, and what they make with loving care, when matured in oak casks, is called Malt Whisky. Each distillery's Whisky has its own individual flavour and is known by the name of the distillery, not by a brand name. The well known and widely distributed brands of Whisky are mixtures ('blends') of many Malt Whiskies and Grain Whisky. Grain Whisky is a comparatively uninteresting and characterless Whisky made by a highly efficient and economical method perfected about 1831; its main ingredients are maize, unmalted and malted barley. There are about fifteen Grain Distilleries in Scotland and their total output is larger than that of the 100 or so Malt Distilleries.

Certain Malt Distilleries have great eminence because their Whisky is especially distinguished and well rounded in flavour. In offering you a short selection of fine Malts, we do so with humility, because we know that there are many others which space forces us to omit. Drink and enjoy them as a fine liqueur or with Schweppes' Malvern water and, maybe, you will never drink a three-star brandy again!

GLENFIDDICH. 70° Proof.	52/6
William Grant. Dufftown.	
GLENMORANGIE. 70° Proof 10 years old	52/6
Macdonald & Muir. Tain.	
GLEN MHOR. 75° Proof. 10 years old	56/–
Mackinlay & Birnie. Inverness.	
HIGHLAND PARK. 75° Proof. 12 years old	58/6
James Grant. Kirkwall. Orkneys.	
THE GLENLIVET. 80° Proof. 12 years old	62/–
George & J. G. Smith. Glenlivet.	
SPRINGBANK. 80° Proof. 12 years old	62/6
J. & A. Mitchell. Campbeltown.	
MACALLAN. 80° Proof. 1946 Make.	65/–
J. Kemp. Craigellachie.	

March 1966

Wein und Wien

To Baron Johann Pasqualati   Vienna, March 1827
Esteemed Friend!
Please send me some more stewed cherries today, but cooked
quite simply, without any lemon. Further, a light pudding, almost
like gruel, would give me great pleasure. My good cook is not yet
competent to provide me with invalid diet. I am allowed to drink
champagne; but please send me a champagne glass as well with
your first delivery. Now about wine. At first Malfatti said it
should only be Moselle. But he declared that there was no pure
Moselle to be had in Vienna. So he himself gave me several bottles
of Krumpholz Kirchner[1] and declared that this was the best wine
for my health, as it was impossible to obtain any genuine Moselle
– Forgive me for giving you so much trouble; You must ascribe
this in part to my helpless condition.

With kind regards, your friend
Beethoven
Autograph in Nationalbibliothek, Vienna

Austrian Wine

GUMPOLDSKIRCHNER SPÄTLESE   13/6
*A full-bodied sweetish wine with a flavour which suggests honey from the
district of Baden.*

KREMZER RIESLING   11/6
An elegant dryish wine from the Kremms area west of Vienna.

Moselle

GRAACHER, 1963   13/–
A crisp, well balanced fruity wine, not too dry.

Rhine

HAMBACHER GRAIN, Upper Palatinate 1963   12/6
A sweetish wine of fine flavour and bouquet.

Chilling: The charm of inexpensive Austrian and German
wines is in their youth and freshness. Do not kill their delicate
flavour by serving them too cold.
1965

[1] i.e. Gumpoldskirchner.

41

The Food for March

'Your bunch of parsley should be a generous one, about the size of a bunch of violets.' One cookery writer, one only, could have written that sentence – Dr Edouard de Pomiane, a man unique among French gastronomic authors. Greatly loved by his public, if not unanimously approved by professionals and orthodox gourmets, this ex-Institut Pasteur professor has, all his working life, been a little bit the *enfant terrible* of French gastronomy. Now in his mid-eighties, Dr de Pomiane has never hestitated to direct an irreverent eye on tradition when he thinks it incompatible with sense, nor to puncture here and there the over-inflated reputation of an established dish: sauce blanche . . . this is a horrible sauce; – homard à l'américaine . . . is a cacophony . . . it offends a basic principle of taste'.

Dr de Pomiane's highly developed critical sense makes him also the most constructive and instructive of writers. Every recipe he gives seems newly created, as fresh as that bunch of violets so surprisingly evoked in connection with a sauce for boiled beef. Above all, Dr de Pomiane is the master exponent of the charms of authentically primitive and simple cooking.

Of a dish from the Swiss mountains M. de Pomiane observes that it is 'a peasant dish, rustic and vigorous. It is not everybody's taste. But one can improve upon it. Let us get to work.' Of the way in which Dr de Pomiane thinks we should go to work improving a primitive dish to our taste while preserving its character intact, this same recipe provides an impeccable example. Does he, as an enthusiastic amateur, add olives and a garnish of parsley and peppers? He does not. Does he, in the manner of the classically trained professional, superimpose cream, wine and truffles upon his rustic and vigorous mountain dish? Not he. One unerring touch, one addition, one only, and the trick is done:

TRANCHES AU FROMAGE

'Black bread – a huge slice weighing 5–7 oz. (or four smaller slices cut thick), French mustard, 8 oz. Gruyère.

'The slice of bread should be as big as a dessert plate and nearly 1 inch thick. Spread it with a layer of French mustard and cover the whole surface of the bread with strips of cheese about $\frac{1}{2}$ inch thick.

'Put the slice of bread on a fireproof dish and under the grill. The cheese softens and turns golden brown. Just before it begins to run, remove the dish and carry it to the table. Sprinkle it with salt and pepper. Cut the slice in four and put it on to four hot plates. Pour out the white wine and taste your cheese slice. In the mountains this would seem delicious, but here it is all wrong.

'But you can put it right. Over each slice pour some melted butter. A mountaineer from the Valais would be shocked, but my friends are enthusiastic, and that is good enough for me.'

Truly, of this kind of cookery writing – kindly, sparkling, free from all bombast, creative in the true sense of that ill-used word – there can never be a surfeit. (I beg readers to try that rustic cheese recipe. And to note the point about spreading the mustard on the bread and underneath the cheese. One such lesson is worth forty volumes of solemn instruction.) It is to be hoped that Peggie Benton, M. de Pomiane's English translator, who has so skilfully rendered his unique prose into English, will eventually produce further translations of de Pomiane books. At the moment two only out of some dozen of his works are available to English readers. It is from these two, *Cooking in 10 Minutes* (1946, reprinted 1956) and *Cooking with Pomiane* (1962) that all my quotations have been taken. Both books are published by Bruno Cassirer of Oxford and distributed by Messrs Faber and Faber. Prices are 12s. 6d. and 18s. od. respectively.

SAUTÉ BANANAS

Cut some bananas into two lengthwise. Fry them in butter for a few minutes. Lift them out and sprinkle them with sugar mixed with a little powdered cinnamon.

ELIZABETH DAVID

STILTON CHEESE

March was a month noted in many a gourmet's diary because it meant the arrival of the first of the season's Stilton cheeses. These were only made between May and September and took around nine months to mature.

Modern methods allow manufacture the whole year round, without, it is claimed, impairing the quality and distinction of this most famous of English cheeses.

M. André Simon, in his *Guide to Good Food and Wines*, quotes a complaint published in 1736 to the effect that Stilton cheeses were not as good as they used to be. The same complaints can be heard today but probably carry even less weight than those made more than two centuries ago. There can be no uniformity in a product so individual as a cheese, but our modern creameries assist purchasers by having their Stiltons graded and labelled 'Extra Selected', 'Selected' and 'Graded'.

Stilton cheese matures best at winter temperatures (40–50°F) and contrary to many beliefs will keep better under mild refrigeration than in a warm room or cupboard where they may lose characteristic moisture and softness.

Some say that a Stilton may be cut horizontally in stepped wedges and that using a scoop is wasteful and unnecessary. Myself, I dig Stilton.

GEORGE VILLIERS

A Dinner in March

All I ask is that it be easy to do. And I can't spend all day cooking. And it must look sensational. And taste exquisite. And I refuse to be doing something messy in the kitchen while everyone else is drinking. And it has got to be original – one is so sick of Chicken à la Crème and the indomitable mousse. And what with everyone dieting, and George Brown going on so, and Lent upon us, one is ridden with guilt if it is at all rich or expensive'.

I doubt if there is any complete answer. But my menu for March should very nearly silence this familiar wail, even if it does mean two hours' work.

LEEKS VINAIGRETTES

For six people: nine small leeks; Vinaigrette dressing made with six tablespoonfuls of olive oil, 1½ tablespoonfuls wine vinegar, a squeeze of lemon, a small clove of garlic (crushed), a tablespoonful of chopped parsley, black pepper, salt and a pinch of sugar.

Cut the green part off the leeks, trim the root, taking care not to remove too much because if the root is cut right off the leek will unravel during cooking. Split the leeks lengthwise and wash well. Poach them in salted water until just tender. (It is a good idea to use a roasting tin instead of a saucepan as the leeks can then be laid side by side, and easily lifted out with a fish slice.) Drain them well on a tea towel. When they are quite dry and cool, arrange them, cut side up, on a serving dish or on individual plates, and spoon over the vinaigrette dressing. Chill slightly before serving.

KIDNEY CASSEROLE

For six people: six lamb's kidneys, six pork chipolata sausages, a dozen button mushrooms, six tiny onions, 2 tablespoonfuls sherry, 1½ cups stock, bayleaf, thyme, rosemary, a small carton sour cream, 1 oz. each of butter and flour, butter for frying.

Skin the kidneys, halve them and remove the core. Fry them quickly in the butter until they are brown, then put them on to a plate. Now fry the sausages, then the onions (peeled but left whole) and then the mushrooms. Put the sausages, onions and mushrooms into a casserole. Pour off the blood that will have run from the kidneys (it can be very bitter) and add the kidneys to the casserole. Pour over the sherry and stock, and add the bayleaf and a pinch of thyme and rosemary.

Cover and cook for one hour in a moderate oven. When the onions and kidneys are tender, dish the meat and vegetables, remove the bayleaf and thicken the sauce with the ounce of butter and ounce of flour worked together. Whisk the sauce to prevent lumps forming, and boil up briefly. Add salt and pepper, and the sour cream. Stir, but do not boil, then pour over the kidney dish.

Mashed potatoes or plain boiled rice mop up the sauce well, and a few triangles of fried bread around the dish look attractive and have a pleasant contrasting crunchiness.

WALNUT PANCAKES

For six people: Fry twelve paper-thin pancakes and keep them wrapped in a tea towel. Coarsely grate or crush with a rolling pin ½ lb. shelled walnuts. Mix these with 4 tablespoonfuls of sugar and a teaspoonful each of cinnamon and nutmeg. Sprinkle each pancake with lemon juice, and roll up with a spoon of the walnut filling inside. Lay the pancakes on a heatproof dish, sprinkle well with lemon and sugar and warm through in the oven before serving. They are very good by themselves, or served with whipped sweetened cream, into which has been folded a little whipped egg white.

PRUDENCE LEITH

Sea food

For the fortunate, cooking is a special, recurring pleasure, both stimulating and relaxing. It is just as rewarding to me in March, when Lent falls and I am thinking of meals without meat. A true cook experiments and widens her repertoire all the time, to please herself and her family, and not just for special seasons or special guests. The two dishes I have chosen are all favourites and are immensely useful for incorporating into Lenten meals.

SCALLOPS

This neglected shellfish is in good condition in March. It is quick to cook and delicious to eat.

Allow two scallops per person for a substantial first course and have the fishmonger remove them from their shells. Scallops are better served on individual fireproof dishes than precariously balanced on their own shells which afterwards clutter up the kitchen. For four people the other ingredients are 4 oz. butter, ½ lb. mushrooms, four tablespoonfuls white wine, one egg yolk, one small teaspoonful arrowroot, ¼ pint double cream, salt and pepper, 4 tablespoonfuls lightly browned crumbs and a little parsley to garnish.

Cut each scallop in half to give two rounds and reserve the coral. Melt half the butter in a saucepan and cook the scallops for about five minutes turning them once. Add the coral and continue cooking for two minutes. Pour in the wine, heat and set alight. At the same time sauté the wiped sliced mushrooms in the remaining butter in a separate pan. Beat the egg yolk with the arrowroot and stir in the cream. Pour this over the scallops, adding the mushrooms and their juices. Taste and season. Stir over gentle heat to thicken and pour into little dishes. Scatter each with breadcrumbs and brown quickly under a hot grill. Dust with parsley and serve immediately.

MUSSELS

These gorgeous little creatures take longer to prepare, but are well worth the trouble, both to see and taste.

For four people allow 3 quarts and see that the mussels are alive by pinching the shells that are open and watching them shut. Put them in a large bowl of cold water, covered with a clean, damp, tea towel sprinkled with cooking salt, for two hours. Now scrub and scrape them vigorously under running water and beard them. Discard any that are open or broken. Leave them in a colander under running water while you prepare the sauce. For this you will need 4 tablespoonfuls olive oil, two cloves garlic, two onions, two pimentos, red and green, 1 lb. peeled, seeded tomatoes, 2 cupfuls of soft breadcrumbs, 1 cupful parsley, squeeze lemon juice, salt and freshly ground black pepper. Melt the crushed garlic and sliced onions in oil in a large deep fireproof casserole that can be brought to the table. Add the seeded, sliced peppers and the prepared tomatoes. After half an hour of gentle cooking stir in the breadcrumbs and the parsley and season with lemon juice, salt and pepper. Have the sauce very hot. Now put all the prepared mussels into a large saucepan with half a bottle of white wine. Cook over a good flame, turning the mussels about with a wooden spoon until they open. Discard any that don't. Quickly and carefully remove the empty half shell from each and drop the full half shells into the fragrant sauce. Strain the wine and mussel juices through muslin into the casserole and serve immediately with a ladle on to soup plates. It is a great help to have two people in the kitchen to open the mussels: speed is important as the mussels will go hard if they are recooked in the sauce. This is a lovely, messy, filling dish.

JEAN GARRETT

An etymological inexactitude . . .

'Palestine soup!' said the Reverend Doctor Opimian, dining with his friend Squire Gryll; 'a curiously complicated misnomer. We have an excellent old vegetable, the artichoke, of which we eat the head; we have another of subsequent introduction, of which we eat the root, and which we also call artichoke, because it resembles the first in flavour, although, me judice, a very inferior affair. This last is a species of the helianthus, or sunflower genus of the Syngenesia frustranea class of plants. It is therefore a girasol, or turn-to-the-sun. From this girasol we have made Jerusalem, and from the Jerusalem artichoke we make Palestine soup.'

MR GRYLL 'A very good thing, Doctor.'

THE REVEREND DOCTOR OPIMIAN 'A very good thing; but a palpable misnomer.'

THOMAS LOVE PEACOCK *Gryll Grange*

. . . *but a very good thing*

For six persons: 2 pints chicken or vegetable stock; 1½ lb. peeled Jerusalem artichokes; two onions, chopped; two leeks (both green and white parts); Bouquet garni (sprig parsley, thyme, stick celery, half bayleaf); two egg yolks; ½ pint thin cream; seasoning; 2 oz. butter.

Melt butter in a large saucepan and soften the onions and sliced leeks in it without browning. Add sliced potatoes and sliced artichokes with the stock and seasoning. Add bouquet garni, cover, and simmer gently for 30 minutes. Pass soup through a sieve or mouli. Pour back into rinsed-out saucepan. Beat yolks with cream. Pour a little of the hot soup on to the cream mixture and stir. Pour this back into the soup, stirring all the time. Reheat carefully, without allowing to boil. Taste and adjust seasoning.

PRUDENCE LEITH

BAKED SOLE WITH PARSLEY BUTTER

Sole is a fish which is subjected to so many fanciful and complicated methods of cooking that it is quite a revelation to find how excellent is a fine whole sole quite plainly and simply cooked.

Unfortunately the two simple methods most suitable for sole, that is, plain grilled or à la meunière, are neither of them entirely practical for the ordinary household. In the first case not many people have a grill large enough to cook more than one rather small sole at a time and in the second it is a question not only of a frying pan sufficiently roomy for more than one fish, but also of the amount of butter needed. Few housewives (or for that matter, restaurant cooks) appear to be able to bring themselves to use the lavish quantity of fresh foaming butter which should be poured over a sole meunière immediately before serving, and without which it simply is not sole meunière at all. So try this method, a version of the French sole sur le plat.

When you buy the soles ask the fishmonger to skin them on both sides, but have the skins wrapped up with your fish. Put these skins into a saucepan and just cover them with water; season very sparingly and put in a couple of sprigs of parsley. Simmer this mixture gently until only 3 or 4 tablespoonfuls of liquid remain.

D

49

Butter a wide shallow fireproof baking dish, put in the fish, over them pour the strained liquid, cover with a piece of buttered greaseproof paper or foil, cook in a very moderate oven, gas No.3, 330°F allowing fifteen minutes for medium-sized sole weighing about ¾ lb. each. Remove the paper, spoon the liquid over the fish, put the dish under the grill for a few seconds until it has acquired a shiny glaze. Serve with a little parsley butter melting over each fish. Allow ½ oz. of butter, a tablespoonful of very finely chopped parsley and a drop or two of lemon juice for each person.

If you do not have a dish large enough for whole soles, then the same method can be applied to fillets, allowing ten minutes cooking time instead of fifteen.

More Food for March

BONED AND ROLLED LAMB WITH KIDNEYS

This is a very straightforward and manageable little joint, simplicity itself to cook and carve.

Ask the butcher to bone and roll a piece of kidney end of loin of lamb, putting in the centre the defatted and sliced kidney, with an extra one if possible so that when the meat is carved there will be a little piece of kidney in each slice. Don't forget to take the bones and trimmings with the meat.

For a little joint weighing about 2 lb. before boning, which will be enough for four people, proceed as follows: rub salt and a little thyme or marjoram into the meat. Put it into a baking tin surrounded by the bones and the trimmings. If you like the flavour of garlic with lamb, put an unpeeled clove underneath the joint. In this way you get the flavour without actually eating the bulb itself. Add 2 teacupfuls of water.

Cook uncovered in a moderately hot oven. Gas No. 5 380°F for about fifty minutes to an hour, depending on the thickness of the meat, and also upon how thoroughly cooked you like it.

Remove the bones, trimmings and garlic. Pour off the juices into a saucepan and leave the meat in the lowered oven to keep hot.

Pour off excess fat from the juices. Reduce the remainder a little by rapid boiling, and serve it separately in a sauce boat.

With the lamb serve, in the summer, either baby carrots or

turnips, or a purée made from very young broad beans, pods and all, or nicely buttered new potatoes. In the winter stewed white haricot beans or a purée of potatoes and Jerusalem artichokes make good accompaniments to lamb.

If you need to cook a larger joint, bear in mind that it is the thickness of the meat rather than its weight which counts when calculating the cooking time, so that a piece which weighs, let us say, nearly twice as much as the one described will not need much more than an extra fifteen to twenty minutes cooking, but it will need rather more liquid in the pan.

ROAST CHICKEN WITH TARRAGON STUFFING

For a roasting chicken weighing about 2½ lb. when dressed and drawn the ingredients for the stuffing are 1 oz. of breadcrumbs, 2 oz. of butter, 2 tablespoonfuls of chopped fresh tarragon, a scrap of garlic, a little strip of lemon peel, salt, pepper, one egg. For roasting the chicken, about 1½ oz. of butter.

Work the breadcrumbs into the softened butter; add the tarragon, the crushed garlic (it should go without saying that you leave this out if you do not like it), the very finely chopped lemon peel, seasonings and the beaten egg. Stuff the chicken. Coat it lavishly with butter. Place it on its side in a baking tin and cover the exposed side with buttered paper or foil. Put in the centre of a preheated and hot oven, gas No. 6, 400°F and cook it altogether for just about an hour, turning it over three times at regular intervals, basting it with the juices in the pan and using a little more melted butter if necessary. For the final five minutes turn the bird breast upwards so that it browns evenly.

The buttery juices in the pan are the only sauce necessary, for the chicken itself will be juicy and moist and full of flavour, but if you like extra gravy, make it from the giblets of the bird previously stewed very gently for a couple of hours with a carrot, a chopped tomato, a sprig or two of tarragon, seasonings, and just enough water to cover.

The nicest accompaniments to roast chicken are a straightforward green salad and perhaps a few plainly cooked new potatoes.

ELIZABETH DAVID

BAKED APPLES

For four people allow eight large Granny Smiths or Cox's, 4 oz. butter, 2 oz. castor sugar, 1 teaspoonful cinnamon, 1 teaspoonful grated lemon rind, 4 oz. raisins, one large glass white wine, 4 tablespoonfuls apricot jam, water to dilute, 4 tablespoonfuls icing sugar, ½ pint single cream.

Carefully peel and core the apples. Butter eight little strips of greaseproof paper big enough to go round each apple and reaching about an inch above each. Cream together the butter and sugar and add the cinnamon, lemon rind and raisins. Wrap apples in paper cases, pack into shallow fireproof dish and fill apple cavities with stuffing. Pour white wine over apples and bake for forty-five minutes at gas No. 3, 325°F until soft but still firm. Melt the apricot jam in a saucepan with a little water and pour in the wine from cooking the apples. Let this bubble and amalgamate and then spoon over the apples from which you have removed the paper cases. Cover each apple thickly with icing sugar and set under a very fierce grill until caramelized. Serve with lots of cream.

JEAN GARRETT

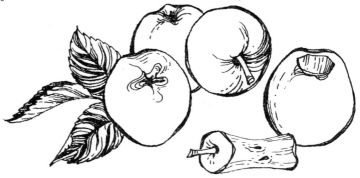

Wine hints and suggestions

For the dinner in March I see that I recommended Amontillado Sherry with the Leeks Vinaigrettes, Mercurey, Clos des Corvées 1961 with the Kidney Casserole and Tawny Port (chilled), with the Walnut Pancakes.

I believe that a strongly flavoured fortified wine is needed to compete with the vinaigrette dressing and the flavour of leeks. Red wine is an obvious choice with the kidneys, and I think it is worth your while to find a wine from the Côte Chalonnaise, where they make some wines just as good, but not so popular in name, as those from their more famous neighbour at Beaujolais, and Mercurey is one of the best. Chilled tawny port, and it must be chilled, and not ruby, should make an intriguing combination with the walnuts in the pancake mixture.

Maybe you will not agree with my suggestions. But I do hope they will provoke, at least, other ideas or thoughts.

Sancerre, one of the best white wines from the Loire Valley, lies in the department of Cher. The wine is dry, but fragrant and tender, and should be drunk young and lightly chilled. 'Pour out the white wine and taste your cheese,' says Doctor Edouard de Pomiane, and my mouth waters at the recollection of his 'Tranches au Fromage' washed down by a bottle of Sancerre.

The red wines of Touraine have a clearly defined bouquet and flavour; the intense smell and taste of the Cabernet grape pervades them. Bourgeuil, north of the river Loire and some thirty miles west of Tours, produces a more robust wine than its neighbour at Chinon. Either of these two interesting red wines are worthy to accompany the Loin of Lamb with Kidneys.

In 1959 I recommended a Rhine Wine, Rudesheimer Kiesel 1955 with the Baked Sole with Parsley Butter. The price was only 12s. od. the bottle! Which comes as a bit of a shock, when you look at today's prices of a similar wine.

Lastly, if you enjoy the taste of your regular brand of blended Scotch Whisky and have never ventured into the land of 100 per cent pure Malt Whisky aged in sherry casks, then you are in for a startling surprise – the difference between chalk and cheese in my opinion. Increased taxation in almost every Budget since 1966 has made these old Malt Whiskies into a luxury, but they are still cheaper than a liqueur Cognac – provided, of course, you enjoy a liqueur Malt Whisky. Do give one of them a trial. If you wish to dilute them, just add a touch of Schweppes Malvern water, never soda-water or tap water.

April

First summer-feeling day . . . The banks are 'versed' with
primroses, partly scattered, partly in plots and squats, and
at a little distance shewing milkwhite or silver – little
spilt till-fulls of silver. I have seen them reflected in green
standing farmyard water.

GERARD MANLEY HOPKINS 1871

The cruellest month?

Awake the land is scattered with light, and see,
Uncanopied sleep is flying from field and tree:
And blossoming boughs of April in laughter shake.

ROBERT BRIDGES 1844–1930

April, from the Latin *aperire*, to open, is the month of budding, and in the French Republican Calendar was called Germinal (the time of budding, 21st March to 19th April). The months of April and May are the crucial and busy periods for everyone connected with the Wine Trade, from the grower to the merchant who buys, imports and bottles his own wine.

We keep our fingers crossed that late frosts will not damage the vines and the prospects of a plentiful harvest in 1965, and at the same time raise the price asked for the 1964 wines.

We travel to France to taste the wines of the previous year, which will have received their first racking (drawn off their lees) and will have had time to settle down after this important operation. No merchant in his senses would venture an honest opinion on the merits of the 1964 vintage at an earlier date, and any purchases made before the spring racking must be a matter of guess work or a gamble.

This is also the time when we make our first offer of the 1962 vintage, which we bottled in the autumn of 1964, to those of our customers who maintain a cellar and like to buy young wines for the future. After a careful tasting we have chosen two inexpensive wines from Bordeaux and Burgundy which we think are wonderful value for money and which you will enjoy drinking in three to four years time.

CH. LES PETITS ARNAUDS, Blaye 1962	9/-
CH. LES HOMMES CHEVAL BLANC, Bourg 1962	11/6
COTES DE BEAUNE 1962	12/6
SAVIGNY LES BEAUNE 1962	13/6

April 1965

56

Who needs a valet?

Il n'y a point de héros pour son valet de chambre
MME CORNUEL *Lettres de Mlle Aissé*

Nothing is more depressing than the conviction that one is not a hero.
GEORGE MOORE *Ave*

Claret is the liquor for boys, port for men; but he who aspires to be a hero must drink brandy.
SAMUEL JOHNSON *Letters to Boswell*

The conviction that I am not a hero does not depress me, because we all have our private heroes in whose deeds we participate in our imagination. At the age of ten it was Beatty, that dashing naval officer, who was my hero. At school I worshipped at the shrine of cricket and it was Strudwick, Hobbs, Parkin and Hendren, not forgetting Charlie Williams, the greatest of all racquet players.

At Sandhurst, my drill instructor C.S.M. Peters, my adjutant 'Boy' Browning and Joe Dudgeon, that supreme horseman, inspired my hero worship. At tennis I was Borotra, the bounding Basque, and at golf I imagined myself as that unique and poker-faced Bobby Locke; shall I ever forget his second shot to the eighteenth green at St Andrews when he needed a four for his fifth Open Championship!

Throughout the years, generals, jockeys, authors, prelates and actors, too numerous to mention, have jostled each other for a place in my heroic life; but only one politician, our national hero Winston Churchill, who was also Colonel of my regiment and my family hero, gained admittance. Auctioneers and toastmasters have excited my imagination, but it is to conductors of symphony orchestras that I have been most faithful. Who amongst us has not wished to stand in their shoes and receive, with that air of humility or disdain, the plaudits of the audience?

In the wine trade I have listened to such heroic masters as Ian Campbell, Willie Byass and Charles Hasslacher and learned that a lifetime is too short to gain all the knowledge which entitles one to speak with authority on the fascinating subject of wine. The thrill of discovery never ceases, when eye, nose and mouth tell one, unmistakably, that here in the glass is nectar fit for a hero and for us poor mortals, whether it be for now or the future.

Incidentally, 100 years ago another hero, Dr Barnardo, founded his first home, in Stepney, for destitute children: here was a man of truly heroic courage, faith and determination.

Claret for Boys

CH. GAZIN, Pomerol 1945   80/–
A perfect example of this superb vintage   (magnum) 160/–

CH. DUCRU BEAUCALILLOU, St Julien 1959   32/–
Has the hallmark of greatness to come

Port for Men

GRAHAM 1963   23/–
A present for the younger generation

Brandy for Heroes

GRANDE FINE CHAMPAGNE COGNAC 1948   126/–
Landed 1949, bottled 1966, obscuration Nil, 33. 6 U.P.

April 1966

Addict – verb, '*to devote or apply habitually to a practice*'. *1577*.
OXFORD ENGLISH DICTIONARY

It was in 1909 that the noun 'addict' was included in the *Oxford English Dictionary* as 'One who is addicted to the habitual and excessive use of a drug or like'. For those of us who have had the remotest contact with addicts to drugs or alcohol the word conjures up a world of human suffering which compels one to compassion for, and understanding of, such grievous afflictions. As a lay member of the Society for the Study of Addiction to Alcohol and other Drugs I know the wonderful work this Society does to seek for the alleviation or cure of such victims.

Luckily most of us are able to practise a variety of addictions which give us much harmless pleasure. In fact my own habitual and weekly addiction transports me, a town dweller, into the English countryside to participate in the lives of a host of old friends; and just at this time I would like to be able to help Jack Archer, who is dangerously near becoming an addict to the whisky bottle. There! My secret is out! The Archers are my addiction, even though I have only known them four years, while many of you may have first met them twenty years ago.

Anyway, Brigadier Winstanley has my full approval when he offers Carol Tregorran and Ralph Bellamy a bottle of Muscadet as an aperitif before lunch and tells them they will continue to drink the same wine with the fish course. Ralph Bellamy, not one of my favourite characters, makes such a sensible criticism when he remarks 'Delicious! Not one of those dry wines which make your face wrinkle up like a squashed lemon!'

Just now I do not want to talk of Muscadet but of Chablis – because, of all dry white wines in the world, Chablis is one of, if not the greatest of all; and though, like Beaujolais, it is more 'imitated' than any other dry white wine in the world, it remains serenely inimitable. Druitt said that 'its flintiness was such an incentive to appetite that it would tempt a man to eat carrion crow'. Under its pale greenish colour and subtle bouquet lurks considerable body with a clean, pebbly flavour. If you have never tasted any of the choicest growths of Chablis, I am confident of your addiction to any, if not all, of the quartet listed below. Alas! These inimitable wines are small in quantity and therefore costly – but hugely rewarding to the palate. Drink them, or keep them and they will grow old gracefully.

CHABLIS GRAND CRU, LES PREUSES, 1966	34/3
CHABLIS PREMIER CRU, VAULORENT, 1966	30/9
CHABLIS PREMIER CRU, VAILLONS, 1966	30/9
CHABLIS GRAND CRU, VAUDÉSIR, 1966	26/3

April 1968

1564   *William Shakespeare*   *1964*

'*A good sherris-sack hath a two-fold operation in it. It ascends me into the brain: dries me there all the foolish and dull and crudy vapours which environ it; makes it apprehensive, quick forgetive, full of nimble fiery and delectable shapes, which, deliver'd o'er to the voice, the tongue, which is the birth, becomes excellent wit. The second property of your excellent Sherris is, the warming of the blood; which, before cold and settled, left the liver white and pale, which is the badge of pusillanimity and cowardice: but the sherris warms it and makes it course from the inwards to the parts extreme. It illumineth the face, which, as a beacon, gives warning to all the rest of this little kingdom, man, to arm; and then the vital commoners and inland petty spirits muster me all to their captain, the heart, who, great and puffed up with this retinue, doth any deed of courage; and this valour comes of sherris. So that skill in the weapon is nothing without sack, for that sets it awork; and leaning, a mere hoard of gold kept by a devil till sack commences it and sets it in act and use.*

Henry IV Part 2 IV iii.

AMOROSO SHERRY

A sherry of unique quality which gains its special character from being unblended and aged in cask for fourteen years: we have just bottled this wine in honour of the 400th anniversary of Shakespeare's birth. The wine will continue to improve in bottle for many years.

AMOROSO SHERRY   35/-

. . . some pigeons, Davy, a couple of short-legged hens, a joint of mutton, and any pretty little tiny kickshaws, tell William cook . . .

Henry IV Part 2 V i

Even allowing for Justice Shallow's anxiety to suit Falstaff's appetite, the menu would seem by present-day standards excessive. The pigeons alone would satisfy most of us: especially cooked *en daube*, a method particularly suited to making the best of these inexpensive and underrated birds.

PIGEONS EN DAUBE

For each person lightly brown in butter two small trussed and drawn pigeons. Transfer the birds to a daubière[1] or terrine and surround them with small onions and button mushrooms, also lightly cooked in butter. Cover each pigeon with two rashers of lightly cooked back bacon. Add to the butter in which the pigeons have been browned a small glass of brandy and a wine glass of red wine. Let this sauce simmer for a few moments then pour over the contents of the terrine. Add seasoning, bouquet garni, a small cupful of stock and a peeled tomato. Cover and seal the pot. Pigeons, at least in England, are not now reared for the table and the British woodpigeons requires slow and gentle cooking: for four pigeons not less than ninety minutes in a very moderate oven.

With this dish we recommend:

NUITS ST GEORGES, 1959   15/-

Be kind and courteous to this gentleman;
Hop in his walks and gambol in his eyes;
Feed him with apricocks and dewberries,
With purple grapes, green figs and mulberries...

A Midsummer-Night's Dream II iii

COMPOTE D'ABRICOTS

It may be doubted whether in Shakespeare's day and even in fairyland, ripe apricots, dewberries, purple grapes and mulberries were available on Midsummer Day. The present-day, year-round, air-freighted and deep frozen availability of practically everything has deprived us of relishing food peculiarly in season. But dried fruit can have its own particular merits especially, perhaps, dried Smyrna apricots. Plump and toothsome as packed, a half-pound steeped overnight in a syrup of three quarters of a pint of water and a quarter pound of white sugar form the succulent equivalent of one and a half pounds of fresh fruit. Add a vanilla pod to the liquid and simmer until the fruit is

[1] For a description, see Elizabeth David's 'French Provincial Cooking.'– Ed.

61

soft. Take out the apricots and, after reducing the liquid to a thickish syrup, remove the vanilla pod and pour over the fruit. Cool in the refrigerator. Serve very cold with cream or a strictly modest libation of Kirsch.

With this sweet we recommend a superb wine from Alsace. Drink it lightly chilled.

MUSCAT RÉSERVE EXCEPTIONELLE, 1961 estate bottled   21/–
April 1964

Food for April

Among a large number of published receipt and housekeeping books which we owe to the industry and the interest in cookery shown by the châtelaines of our country houses and the ladies of our aristocracy (one of the earliest was the Countess of Kent's *A True Gentlewoman's Delight*, 1653, the latest Lady Arabella Boxer's *First Slice Your Cookbook*, 1964) the *Cookery Book* of Lady Clark of Tillypronie is the most impressive in size and in content. This immense book, compiled and edited by Miss C. F. Frere, from a half-dozen massive manuscript notebooks left by Lady Clark, was published in 1909, some nine years after Lady Clark's death.

Miss Frere observes that 'so great is the variety of locality from which the recipes were drawn, that Lady Clark may be said to have focused much of the best cookery of Europe in her collection'. Certainly Lady Clark's recipes, noted down over a period of fifty years, bear witness to the cosmopolitan character of English cooking in the four or five decades preceding 1914.

Although, as is inevitable in books compiled from cookery notebooks, Lady Clark's recipes are often sketchy, it is for the ideas and the feeling of authenticity, for the certainty that these recipes were actually used and the dishes successful – or they would not have been recorded – that the book is valuable.

The following recipes are among scores recorded by Lady Clark as having been used in her own kitchens at Birk Hall and Tillypronie, the Aberdeenshire estates where she and Sir John Clark lived.

LOBSTER OR CRAB SOUP

Quantities for three ample helpings are:
1 oz. butter, one leek, two sticks of celery including leaves, about
¼ lb. each of green peas (shelled weight) and spinach, half a small
fresh cucumber, seasoning, 1 pint of water, ¼ pint of mild clear
veal or chicken stock, a small quantity, say about two heaped
tablespoonfuls, of cooked crab or lobster meat.

In a soup pot melt the butter. Put in first the cleaned and chopped leek together with the cucumber, unpeeled and coarsely
grated, and the sliced celery. Add the peas and cleaned spinach.
After ten minutes gentle cooking and 1 dessertspoonful of salt, and
a lump of sugar. Cook for another fifteen minutes. Sieve through
the fine mesh of the mouli or reduce to a purée in the blender.

Return this purée to the saucepan. Add the stock and the crab
or lobster meat. Heat gently. Season with nutmeg.

Quantities, method and timing in this recipe are my own, but it
is evident, from Lady Clark's note, that her cook used crab or
lobster left over from another dish. This addition was perhaps an
afterthought, the basic soup being simply a vegetable purée,
rather thin and of a pleasing clear green with a good fresh flavour.

Another of the specialities from Lady Clark's own kitchen is an
after dinner savoury of cheese biscuits to be eaten hot from the
oven.

THICK PARMESAN BISCUITS

For a dozen biscuits: ¼ lb. plain flour, 2 oz. each of butter, and
grated Parmesan, the yolk of one egg, salt, cayenne pepper.

Rub the butter into the flour, add the cheese, egg and seasonings. Roll out the dough to the thickness of half an inch. Cut into
1 in. diameter rounds. Arrange on a baking sheet. Bake in the
centre or lower centre of a very moderate oven, gas No. 2 or 310–
330°F for just on twenty minutes. Serve hot.

Lady Clark made the point that it is the thickness of these
biscuits that gives them their character. The Parmesan is also
essential. English cheese will not do. The biscuits can be stored in
a tin and heated up when wanted.

Lady Clark is particularly good on fruit dishes. Her method of
making a summer fruit compote is well worth attention.

STRAWBERRY OR RASPBERRY COMPOTE

'Boil up sugar and water, This boiling syrup is poured over the fruit which is piled in a dish. Then the syrup is poured off and reboiled; this is repeated three times; it retains the flavour of fresh fruit without a suspicion of "jamminess".'

As a rough guide, for a pound of fruit use a syrup made of $\frac{1}{4}$ lb. of sugar and $\frac{1}{4}$ pint of water, boiled together for ten minutes. Early raspberries will probably need rather more sweetening. In the winter Lady Clark's method makes a melon compote which turns an otherwise disappointing honey-dew or green-skinned Elche melon into an interesting dessert dish. Flavour the syrup with lemon peel or a vanilla pod.

ELIZABETH DAVID

Spring Food

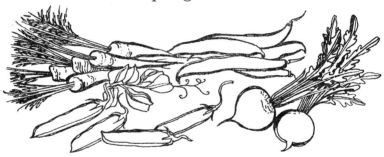

April, month of St George and Shakespeare, sees the beginning of the first gastronomic delights of summer and the first overseas visitors of the season. What is a typical meal to offer them? The best cooking of these islands is never far from that of the farmhouse or manor where it evolved, and our traditional recipes have never been really urbanized, for we are all countrymen at heart.

As our breakfast specialities may not have all been sampled by tourists, a small portion of kedgeree can be a starter. The visitor can be given two novelties in one, if in the usual recipe kippers are used instead of smoked haddock – the kipper fillets now on sale are ideal. For four people, allow one packet of fillets, a breakfast cup ($\frac{1}{4}$ lb.) of rice – the brown Italian is excellent – four chopped hardboiled eggs, and a raw egg and $\frac{1}{4}$ pint of thick cream, to be

64

stirred into the prepared mixture of cooked rice and flaked fish, pepper and lemon juice, about ten minutes before serving.

As a main dish, the roast beef of the country is a 'must'. For those who want a menu for luncheon after sightseeing, a cold joint, marbled pink and white, saves the cook and is just as good as hot. Buttered new carrots or, simplest of all, watercress with a light dressing of lemon juice, salt, pepper and walnut oil (obtainable at Wholefood, Baker Street) partner new potatoes, and if towards the end of the month, the new peas come in from the Canaries or Italy, they can be supreme. For those who are unable to pick them out of their own gardens, peas can disappoint. But here is how to make them succulent enough for the most demanding Frenchman, who thinks that the only way to cook them is with chopped ham and lettuce.

SPRING PEAS

Shell and rinse the peas, but don't let them soak. Measure enough water just to cover them when they are in the saucepan, and in this water put salt, a flat teaspoonful of sugar and bring the water to the boil. As it boils, add a tablespoonful of olive oil, let it come back to the boil and then add the peas, plus mint if liked, though my own preference is for two or three finely sliced pickling onions – the mint can go on the potatoes if you enjoy the flavour. Cover the saucepan, but keep a watch on the peas, as they will cook in a few minutes, absorbing water and oil, and should hardly need draining. Put them in the serving dish with a knob of butter. They will stand long enough for the plates to be changed, but the longer they wait, the more they are likely to wrinkle.

Strawberries and cream are a summer classic. The late Robin Adair, Boulestin's partner, taught me to sprinkle the hulled fruit with a little freshly squeezed orange juice, leave it in a cool place and then listen to the guests debate as to what liqueur had been used. But should the early fruit not be as perfect as one would wish for visitors, a fool – a dish that is peculiar, as far as I can make out, to these islands – is an alternative. The quick-frozen strawberries and raspberries make an acceptable substitute for fresh fruit, providing first-quality double cream is used, and make a delicious change from gooseberry fool.

FOOL SUPREME

For four people, allow ½ lb. each of strawberries and raspberries, 1¼ pints of whipped double cream and a dessertspoonful of fresh orange juice. Sugar is a matter of taste as the fruit is sweet already, and I myself never add any. Put the fruit and orange juice either into a liquidizer or mash it thoroughly, and then sieve it. Fold the fruit into the cream and put in a cool place until required. It seems to taste better if the fruit and cream are not completely combined but, so to speak, swirled together. If packed in the separate compartments of a vacuum jar, this is a good Glyndebourne or river picnic pudding.

PAMELA VANDYKE PRICE

HOT VEGETABLE HORS D'OEUVRES

A lovely first course can be made simply and quite inexpensively of tender spring vegetables. For six people you will need a small cauliflower, a doxen baby carrots, a dozen button onions, six small young turnips, a pound of the first imported broad beans, two good handfuls of new peas, ¼ lb. unsalted butter, 2 tablespoonfuls of sugar and 2 tablespoonfuls of chopped parsley.

Divide cauliflower carefully and peel carrots, onions and turnips, leaving them all whole. Remove strings from beans but leave pods. Shell peas or use frozen ones. Cook vegetables until just tender and drain, reserving only 6 tablespoonfuls water from the turnips. Pour into large sauté pan or paella dish, add butter cut into pieces and the sugar, and season well. Glaze the onions in this turning until well browned. Add all the other vegetables at intervals to slightly brown the turnips and carrots, but taking care not to break beans, peas or cauliflower sprigs. Toss in the parsley and serve with hot French bread.

FISH IN CREAM SAUCE

This is a dish to which to become addicted. It is much more elaborate and contrasts well with the colourful hors d'oeuvres, but requires a certain amount of care and trouble.

Poach 1½ lb. of firm white fish in a good court bouillon until just tender. Drain, skin and set aside, saving the cooking liquor. Open a quart of mussels sprinkled with onion in a glass of white wine. Set aside in the half shell together with cooking liquor strained through muslin. Heat ½ lb. peeled prawns or shrimps in butter and keep warm together with ¼ lb. tinned, frozen or fresh crabmeat.

To make the sauce melt 2 oz. butter in heavy saucepan, blend in 2 oz. flour and cook until straw coloured. Take from flame and stir in the hot liquor from the fish and the mussels, and then about ½ pint hot milk to give you a thick sauce. Beat two egg yolks into ¼ pint double cream in a large bowl and gradually add the hot fish sauce. Return to the pan and continue cooking gently, stirring all the time for five minutes. Season carefully with pepper and a little lemon juice.

Arrange flaked fish, mussels, crabmeat and prawns in a large shallow gratin dish and pour the sauce over. Garnish with six large unshelled prawns. Sprinkle with two tablespoonfuls grated gruyère cheese and 2 oz. butter cut into small pieces. Reheat slowly in a bain-marie and finish by browning under a hot grill. Serve with scrubbed new potatoes and green salad.

Finish the meal with chilled, tender, fresh rhubarb cooked in the oven with a little grated lemon rind. Hand thin cream and small macaroons.

JEAN GARRETT

OEUFS MOLLETS FINES HERBES

Elizabeth David says, 'This is one of those excessively (and deceptively) simple dishes which can make the reputation of a good cook', and I should add, to my cost on one or two occasions, the word 'mar'! This is because the coddling of eggs requires accuracy of timing, so that the whites are quite set and the yolks still just runny, and because the shelling must be done with care and deliberation. Allow two eggs per person, a dessertspoonful of fresh chopped herbs, such as parsley, chives and tarragon, and a tablespoonful of butter.

Put the eggs in boiling water and boil for five minutes (for very small or very large eggs, the timing must obviously be adjusted); take out and cool under the cold tap to arrest the cooking. As you shell each egg, keep them warm in a bowl of warm water. While doing this, have ready a heavy pan, and then sauté the eggs in the melted butter, without letting it burn; sprinkle in the herbs, adding a squeeze of lemon juice, and serve immediately in very hot metal or china egg dishes. Provided the eggs are prepared before hand, and the herbs are ready chopped, they can be made at the last minute.

French Country Cooking

MOUSSE AU CHOCOLAT A L'ORANGE

The reliable formula for chocolate mousse, with the addition of a subtle orange flavour. Break 4 oz. bitter chocolate into squares and put in a fireproof bowl into a low oven. After a few minutes, remove when soft and stir in four well-beaten egg yolks, then 1 oz. softened butter and the juice of one orange – preferably Seville when in season, or, even more preferably, an equivalent amount of Grand Marnier in place of the orange juice. (Miniatures of Grand Marnier can be bought at most off licences.) Beat the four egg whites stiffly as for a soufflé and fold them into the chocolate mixture. Pour into little pots, glasses or coffee-cups (this quantity will fill four to six). Cool in the refrigerator.

French Provicial Cooking

Wine hints and suggestions

There is no doubt that those people who have consistently bought vintage red wines in their infancy and laid them down for future drinking have been amply repaid today. To compare the opening prices of the 1962 clarets, offered in the spring of 1965, with the prices asked for the same wines in 1970 is startling. I admit that the last five years have seen so many increases in the form of duty, freight, insurance, bottling charges and the iniquitous SET that it was inevitable.

Since 1961 there have been thirteen Duty changes alone, so that today about 40 per cent, or say 5s. 4½d., is the duty on an ordinary bottle of table wine. Here is the cost analysis of a bottle of wine retailing at 12s. od. duty 5s. 4½d., bottling, freight, insurance and clearing charges 1s. 9d., internal distribution, sales and promotional costs and trade profit margins 2s. 10½d., value of wine 2s. od. – total 12s. od. Makes you think, doesn't it?

Any good wine merchant will be delighted to advise you on starting a cellar if you can give him an annual sum of money to invest, and many of them have schemes for laying down young wines on 'pay as you go' by Banker's Order. If you have no cellar of your own he will store your wine for a modest sum. If you have friends who will go shares with you in buying the run of a cask of young vintage claret (24 doz. bottles) I know that your merchant will make you a keen price. Even your favourite non-vintage vin ordinaire is worth buying on these terms, and will greatly improve if you can give it time in bottle (say six months), before you begin to drink it.

Collecting individual bottles of wine can also be an absorbing and rewarding hobby if you keep your eyes and ears open, particularly for some of the 'off' vintages. Do not be shy of asking wine merchants if they have any interesting oddments, even single bottles, or bin ends and remnants. Some country hotels, restaurants and local household auctions can also yield some surprises.

May

The ha-ha wall of the orchard is the favourite haunt
of butterflies; they seem to love its sunny aspect, and
often cling to the loose stone like ornaments attached
by some cunning artist. Sulphur butterflies hover here
early in the spring, and later on white and brown and
tiny blue butterflies pass this way, calling en route.
Sometimes a great noble of the butterfly world comes
in all his glory of his wide velvety wings, and deigns to
pause awhile that his beauty may be seen.

RICHARD JEFFERIES 1879

'A propos de bottes'

Those who wish to study the developments and refinements of wine should ignore the ponderous pronouncements of the pundits.

ALLAN SICHEL *Wine*

Today I read that the young French intellectual, Jean-Luc Godard, says 'The British are quite nice, but they're closed up.' This view-point and the wise advice of the late Allan Sichel (his recent death is a great loss to the Wine Trade) reminds me of the wine pundit who, when asked his opinion of a bottle of Ch. Latour 1928 at a luncheon party in 1948, replied 'This wine is completely shut in.' 'Will it ever get out?' asked the wit of the party. 'No, never!' came the answer. How I wish the pundit could have been made to eat his words, some ten years later, when the wine was liberated!

It is the middle of March while I write these notes and I am suffering from election fever. Hundreds of politicians are making ponderous pronouncements about the state of my health and how they will cure me if only I will give them my vote. None of them have told me that, 'Because extra leisure is put before extra effort by too many people of all classes' (*The Times*, 10th March), this might be a reason for my plight today.

Christopher's are part of a nation of small shopkeepers and it happens that we must 'Import or Die'. We work like beavers to preserve our treasured independence, we are proud of our good name and our staff who contribute to so much of the personal service we try to give you. But I can feel on the back of my neck the hot breath of the next Chancellor telling me not to import so much wine, and in the same breath exhorting me to collect his taxes so that he can pay for his election promises! 'Export or Die', and I raise my glass of imported wine to my partner who, by his hard work, patience and skill, has earned those precious dollars for our balance of payments from our first large shipment of Scotch to the USA. Like that bottle of Ch. Latour 1928 it has taken ten years for his efforts to become liberated!

I predict that you will enjoy drinking the following wines in May, but predictably enough I do not know what will happen in the Budget!

72

BROUILLY, Beaujolais 1964   13/6
POUILLY FUISSÉ 1964   14/6
TRAMINER, Alsace 1964   16/–

On every bottle of these wines we have paid 3s. 7d. to the Treasury.

May 1966

'Words, words . . .'

You cram these words into my ears, against the stomach of my sense.

WILLIAM SHAKESPEARE *The Tempest*

If I tell you that, today, I am in a state of euphoria because I have refused to escalate the sales of sophisticated wines, will you understand what I mean? No? Nor do I! From my reading of the daily papers I find the word 'euphoria' (not in the *Oxford Dictionary*) almost always relates to politicians. The *Daily Telegraph* Information Office has enlightened me with a translation from the Greek word *euphos* – 'a state of well being'. I did not ask whether this condition can be escalated by copious draughts of sophisticated wines!

To 'escalate', (not mentioned in the *Oxford Dictionary*), has become a 'dirty' verb which some people use for the express purpose of chastising the efforts of our friends and allies in the Far East. I do find the nouns 'escalade' – 'the scaling of walls with ladders' – and 'escalator' – 'a moving staircase for carrying passengers up or down' – and so I presume that what goes up must come down! And lo and behold! The verb to 'de-escalate' has now appeared in our language.

'Sophisticated' is even more confusing when applied at random to such things as the latest form of lighting on the M4, weapons of war of modern design, and, to my horror wines. A sophisticated person means to me someone who is worldly wise; a sophisticated thing is one that is deprived of simplicity; but a sophisticated wine means that it is adulterated. Wine writers please note!

However, during the month of February I found myself in a state of euphoria on four occasions; firstly after Gerald Moore's Farewell Concert; secondly after watching on television that

73

gentle and unsophisticated man Yehudi Menuhin talking to two of his pupils; thirdly after reading in *The Times* of 21st February 'A Letter from America' signed by seventy-nine distinguished Americans who wish to strengthen and preserve the bonds between our two countries (a letter that would have gladdened the heart of the late Sir Winston Churchill); and fourthly after drinking a well-decanted bottle of Ch. Petrus 1943 (unsophisticated and château bottled!).

Acquired taste?

'I rather like bad wine,' said Mr Mountchesney; 'one gets so bored with good wine'.
DISRAELI *Sybil*, Book I, Ch. I

'Good' wine is too readily accepted as being synonomous with expensive wine, or wine of a famous name, and whilst this is yet one more example of the brand-consciousness of our present age it is nevertheless quite untrue. Any wine is 'bad' that is badly made, and in an age when demand outstrips the supply of wine there is, alas! far too much bad wine about, both cheap and expensive.

We believe that in many cases the best value in wine is to be found in the cheaper ranges. Little skill is required to buy fine and expensive wine; its qualities are all too apparent. Cheap wine is quite another matter, for the smallest defects become all too obvious after a little time in bottle. The two wines we offer this month represent excellent value for money. Do try them, even if they are from 'unfashionable' districts.

RIOJA, Spanish Red Claret-type
An excellent balanced and fruity wine that compares more than favourably with many so-called Bordeaux wines, and at a price which is striking for its modesty.   7/-
CHATEAU ROUBAUD, Costières du Gard
Grown west of Arles, this is a wine drunk best when young. In style it has much in common with the fruity wines of the lower Rhône, but its elegance makes it an ideal summer red wine.   8/6
May 1964

74

A Menu for May

What shall we have for lunch in May, lunch in May, lunch in May? What shall we have for lunch in May on a cold and frosty morning? So sang I to myself as I prepared to write this article. And then, for the first time in my life, I realized what nonsense we had sung as children. Nuts in May, indeed! What next? as Norman Douglas would have said. How had this folklorique inaccuracy crept into our nurseries? I went to a learned friend. 'Nuts in May', said he, 'is a corruption of knots (or knottes) of may (bouquets of aubépine – Proust's second favourite flower – the first being catteleyas) which children used to gather on May Day (quite likely to be cold and frosty).'

Where, then, for inspiration? Shakespeare, perhaps. But even he gets rather carried away: 'When birds do sing, Hey-ding-a-ding.' Oh! 'sweet-lovers love the spring', so let us have a sweet (I call it a pudding) for sweet-lovers to have with their Château d'Yquem, a gigot with primeurs and a soup made with nuts which you can get in May. This turns out to be a dinner menu, so we still don't know what to have for lunch in May, lunch in May, lunch in May.

PEANUT SOUP

½ lb. shelled peanuts; half large onion; 1 tablespoonful butter; ¾ pint chicken stock; ¼ pint milk; 1 tablespoonful cream; pepper; (sherry).

Skin the nuts and pulverize them. (I do it in a Moulinex.) Chop the onion. Melt the butter. Cook the onion till soft but not coloured. Stir in the nuts and cook for a minute. Add the chicken stock, bring to the boil and simmer for three quarters of an hour. Put through a mill. Add the pepper. Probably no salt required. Add the milk and bring to the boil. Turn off the heat. Add the cream and serve. (If you like, you can add a glass of dry sherry.)

GIGOT AUX PRIMEURS

Get the smallest leg of lamb you can from your butcher. Rub it with garlic and put a piece of garlic into the bone. Heat some olive oil in a baking-tin in a hot oven. Put in some fresh rosemary and on that put the lamb, pouring some more oil on top of it. Cook at No. 7 for ten minutes, then turn the joint over and cook for another ten minutes. Turn the oven down to No. 5. Baste or turn every five minutes. According to size, the joint will take forty to sixty minutes to cook, depending also, of course, on how pink you like it. Season towards the end of its cooking. While it is cooking, cook separately any young vegetables you can find: tiny new potatoes, peas, mange-tout peas, broad beans, baby carrots, asparagus, seakale. Serve the lamb in the middle of a big dish, surrounded by clumps of these primeurs. If you have a silver nutmeg-grater, pass it round for guests to grate some nutmeg on the lamb.

MELON AND GINGER

Take a melon, cut it in half and remove the pips. Cut out the flesh with a large pommes parisiennes cutter. Mix the pieces with pieces about the same size of preserved ginger – half as much ginger as melon. Put in the shell and cover with whipped cream. Decorate with powdered ginger or powdered crystallised violets.

ROBIN MCDOUALL

Fish in May

FILLETS OF BRILL, CHICKEN TURBOT OR JOHN DORY WITH CREAM AND WINE SAUCE

For two fillets of any of these fish the other ingredients are $\frac{3}{4}$ pint of stock (see recipe below) made from the carcase, two large tomatoes, $\frac{1}{2}$ oz. of butter, 4 tablespoonfuls of white wine, 4 to 5 oz. of thick cream, parsley or chives or tarragon, seasonings.

Bake the fillets, covered with fish stock (see recipe below) and a buttered paper in a very moderate oven, gas No. 3, 330°F, for about twenty to twenty-five minutes.

Skin and chop the tomatoes; cook them with the butter in a small pan until the water has evaporated and you have a table-spoonful or two of thickish pulp.

Transfer the cooked fillets to their serving dish, and keep them warm either in a very low oven or over a saucepan of hot water.

Boil the liquid in the baking tin over fast heat until it is reduced by half. Stir in the tomato mixture, then the wine, and finally the cream. Cook quickly, stirring the sauce until the cream has thickened; it should in fact be a little thicker than would appear necessary, because extra liquid will have come from the fillets while they have been waiting, and this must be taken into consideration.

Taste for seasoning. Stir in a little parsley, tarragon, or fresh chives. Pour over the fish.

This is a really beautiful dish, and if you want to make it into a more substantial one, serve with it a little plain boiled rice or tiny new potatoes. In any case there will be ample for four people for a first course, or for two as a main dish. One has to remember that although it may not look it, white fish is very nourishing food.

SIMPLE FISH STOCK

Put the trimmings, head, and carcase of the fish – if it is a large one like brill or John Dory ask the fishmonger to break it up for you – into a saucepan with a peeled onion, a little slice of lemon, a sprig of tarragon or fennel if you have it, a couple of tablespoonfuls of wine vinegar or four of white wine, and about a teaspoonful of salt. You then pour in enough cold water just to cover the contents. Bring it to simmering point and then allow about twenty-five minutes very gentle cooking. Then all you have to do is to strain the stock and measure off the quantity for the recipe.

Never let your fish stock boil fiercely or for a prolonged period or you may get that slightly acrid taste from the bones and skin of the fish (although, of course, much depends upon the variety of fish you are cooking) which characterizes a carelessly made fish soup or sauce. You can always obtain a more concentrated flavour by reducing the stock after it has been strained.

ELIZABETH DAVID

77

Continuing with Red Wine

The average person's cellar often lacks the expensive sweet Sauternes which is the ideal accompaniment to fruit or a pudding. Champagne seems a bit ostentatious. The muscatel type of wine is not everyone's cup of tea. It is sometimes, therefore, more practical to continue for the rest of the meal drinking the claret or burgundy one has been drinking with the meat and to end up with a savoury. But not just any savoury. Scotch woodcock, herring-roes, curried shrimps on toast may be delicious in themselves but they are death to a good red wine. It is better to have cheese.

MARROW-BONES

All too rarely seen these days, marrow-bones were a popular savoury in Edwardian times. Get the butcher to cut them in 7 in. lengths. Make a paste of flour and water and cover each end of the bone (to prevent the marrow running out). Tie each one in a floured cloth. Put them standing up in a deep saucepan of boiling water and boil for forty minutes. Remove the cloth and paste. Wrap a table-napkin round each. Serve with hot, unbuttered toast, a marrow-scoop, salt and cayenne.

If you don't possess any marrow-scoops, you will have to scoop out the marrow with a knife (in the kitchen) and serve it on toast. Alternatively, you can get the butcher to remove the marrow, then you cut it in $\frac{1}{2}$ in. pieces and poach them in boiling water for five minutes and serve them on toast.

MUSHROOM TART

For the pastry: $\frac{1}{2}$ lb. flour, $\frac{1}{4}$ lb. butter, $\frac{1}{4}$ cup water, salt.
For the filling: 1 lb. mushrooms, $\frac{1}{3}$ cupful of cream, one onion, 3 oz. butter, one rasher bacon, salt and pepper.

Sift the flour on to a pastry-board. Make a hollow in the middle, mix in the water, butter (softened) and salt. Knead it to get the ingredients well mixed and leave it all day, covered with a cloth. Roll it out and line a buttered flan-tin with part of it, keeping the other piece for the top.

Chop the bacon and the onion finely and slice the mushrooms;

cook them, separately, in a little butter. When the mushrooms are soft, stir in the cooked bacon and onion. Season. Add the cream and bring to the boil. Put the mushrooms in the tart and put on the rest of the pastry, pinching the edges together and cutting off any surplus. Cook in a moderate oven for thirty to forty minutes.

Any cheese savoury is a good accompaniment to a red wine: one of the many variations of Welsh rarebit; one of the many French variations of quiche au fromage; profiteroles or pots de crème with cheese instead of chocolate; the not-to-be-despised cheese-straws. Best of all, perhaps, is a cheese soufflé, though some connoisseurs say that it is best accompanied by an expensive sweet Sauternes – which gets us back where we started.

ROBIN MCDOUALL

For Miss Jean Brodie

CRÈME BRULÉE

The main point of interest about Messrs Francis Collingwood and John Woollam's *Universal Cook and City and Country Housekeeper*, published in 1791, is the French translation which appeared in Paris in 1810. The flow of English translations of French cookery books has been well-sustained ever since the mid-seventeenth century when La Varenne's celebrated *French Cook* appeared in England. French kitchen terms peppered throughout English cookery books, and half-anglicized names of French dishes are no novelty to us. When for once the tide runs in the reverse direction we get a new view of our own cookery, an insight into the oddness of traditional names as they appear in another language.

In the case of *Le Cuisinier Anglais Universel ou le Nec Plus Ultra de la Gourmandise* there are some interesting metamorphoses. To English ears 'pâté de hachis' does not at all convey our mince pie, however literally correct the translation. Jugged hare oddly becomes 'lièvre lardé'. Batter pudding we find put firmly in its place as 'pudding à la farine', and for hard dumplings we get 'dumpling fermé'.

Some of our cherished specialities defeated the translator,

79

among them 'le catchup' and 'le browning', ('to even the most skilled of French cooks these sauces will be new,' says the publishers preface). The syllabub turns up as Eternal Syllabub, 'syllabub solide', and 'syllabub sous la vache'.

The pen of the French translator give a new aspect to several of our old sweet dishes, among them the trifle which, as 'bagatelle', regains its lost charm. Cheesecakes also return to grace an elegance as 'talmouses.' 'Folie de groseilles vertes' evokes something altogether more giddy and abandoned than a cool and imperturbably English gooseberry fool: and somehow it is difficult to connect 'poulet en capilotade' with that old friend, the 'pulled chicken' of Edwardian breakfasts.

Here and there, a recipe is more familiar under its French than its English title. In the late nineteenth century for example, English Burnt Cream reverted to its old French name of 'crème brûlée', its formula being much as it appeared in the early editions of Massialot's famous *Cuisinier Roial et Bourgeois*, first published in 1691 and translated into English, as the *Court and Country Cook*, in 1702.

The recipe given for Burnt Cream in *The Universal Cook* like a great many in the book, was lifted word for word from Elizabeth Raffald's *Experienced English Housekeeper* of 1769. Our two genial innkeepers, hosts at the London Tavern and at the Crown and Anchor in the Strand, caterers to the Whig Club, and according to their French publisher, cooks to any number of 'riches lords' admitted openly that they had considered it unnecessary to work out their own recipes. The works of John Farley, Hannah Glasse, Charlotte Mason, as well as Elizabeth Raffald had all been pillaged for the *Universal Cook*, so that what in fact French readers were getting was an anthology of eighteenth- and late seventeenth-century English and anglicized French recipes, some of which must have seemed pretty archaic to the Paris of 1810.

The crème brûlée, curiously enough, appears to have already vanished from the repertoire of French cooking by the end of the eighteenth century. Its survival in England seems to have been due to the skill displayed in its confection by the chef in charge of the kitchens of Trinity College Cambridge in the 1890's.

BURNT CREAM

'Boil a pint of cream with sugar and a little lemon-peel shred fine. Beat the yolks of six, and the whites of four eggs separately, and when the cream is cold put in your eggs, with a spoonful of orange-flower water, and one of fine flour. Set it over the fire, keep stirring it till it is thick and then put it into a dish. When it is cold, sift a quarter of a pound of sugar all over it, and brown it with a hot salamander, till it looks like a glass plate put over your cream'.

As far as the cream goes this recipe is excellent – provided only a very little sugar, hardly more than 2 tablespoonfuls goes into the pint of cream. Over-sweetened, and with the addition of that 'glass-plate' of sugar on the top, crème brûlée can become unbearably cloying. It is also to be noted that the English pint of those days was 16 fl. oz. as opposed to our present-day 20 oz. Imperial pint.

When it comes to replacing the obsolete salamander, most cooks nowadays put the sugared cream under a grill, until the sugar has caramelized. For this system an electric grill gives better results than its gas equivalent. Perhaps we need to revive the salamander, which is a thick flat iron plate on the end of a long handle. This instrument was made red hot in the coals, then held immediately over the dish to be glazed or caramelized. For Burnt Cream, a salamander of the precise diameter of the inside of a $1\frac{1}{4}$ pint soufflé dish is the ideal.

ELIZABETH DAVID

Growth of a Wine Lover

Are you a wine lover or merely a wine drinker? Not an easy question to answer because you cannot just pigeon-hole those who drink wine into Philistines and Snobs. I started as a wine drinker and, by good fortune, ended as a wine lover. But it certainly does not happen to us all. Most of us drink wine because we like its taste or because we find it helps us to be friendly and sociable. In any case, you must start to drink wine before you can discover whether you will fall in love with it. Thereafter the period of courtship, from the first groping tastes to the declaration of love, can be just as hazardous as the first flirtations between boy and girl, and whether it leads to a lasting and happy marriage depends on your personal efforts.

As a hard-drinking (and by 'hard' I mean spirit-drinking) subaltern in a Cavalry Regiment in India I never dreamt that I would fall in love with wine, and for that matter, it was equally difficult to imagine, at that time, that I would eventually fall in love with the last five quartets of Beethoven! Except on Guest Nights I drank beer, gin and whisky in that order, and the inevitable glass of Port or Madeira in which to toast my Sovereign.

My first stroke of fortune came in my teens, when my elder sister married a Frenchman from Bordeaux. On my frequent summer visits I was given a powerful injection of good wine, which never quite evaporated during my hard-drinking days. In fact, I can still remember a bottle of Ch. Ducru Beaucaillou 1893 which I drank in 1924 at the Chapon Fin in the company of René Samazeuilh. He had the unique distinction of being decorated for gallantry by the British, with the Distinguished Conduct Medal and the Military Cross, in the Great War. He was my hero: he loved wine, women, horses and golf. What a tutor!

My second piece of luck was slow promotion. I was still a subaltern after ten years service. So, thanks to a brother officer's introduction, I left the Army and joined Christopher's, a step I have never regretted. Thanks to the generosity of my superiors in Christopher's, and of members of the Wine Trade as a whole, from then on I never lacked opportunities to taste wines of every description and quality.

If I tell you that, as a result of the generosity of, and friendship with, one man in the Trade, I drank at luncheon on 30th December 1969 Ch. Lafite 1929, 1893 and 1870, I could expect you to retort 'What a pity he did not wait for the centenary of the 1870.' However, stories and examples of the old and rare wines which you have tasted are, generally speaking, boring to the listener. But I make no apology for this example of what true wine lovers will give to their friends.

Obviously, such strokes of luck as I have enjoyed during my years in the Wine Trade do not come to all wine drinkers. Next month I will set out my Code for Wine Lovers, which I hope will be of help to you in the fascinating hobby of wine tasting, collecting and drinking.

June

Once more I stand by the riverside and look up at the cliff castle towers and mark the wild roses swinging from the crag and watch the green woods waving and shimmering with a twinkling dazzle as they rustle in the breeze and shining of the summer afternoon, while here and there a grey crag peeps from among the tufted trees.

FRANCIS KILVERT 1875

'As soon seek roses in December – ice in June . . .'. Perhaps now that porpoises have been seen in the English Channel, and hoopoes are nesting in the Isle of Wight – both signs, so they say, for a long hot summer – we shall once more have the chance to enjoy all that is best in an English summer. June is the month of punts on the river, meals out of doors, Midsummer Balls . . . of chilled wine and champagne. This month, therefore, we have tempted fate and selected a range of wines which are at their best when chilled and drunk on a warm summer's day. Do be careful to avoid excessive chilling; this only numbs the wine, and masks both its flavour and bouquet.

BIJOU D'ALSACE, 1961
Light, deliciously fresh, and, although grapey, is dry and clean on the palate. Alsace produces some of the best wines for summer drinking and unlike so many wine growing areas, it has had a succession of fine vintages with no increases in the price of its wine.   9/–

PIESPORTER LAY, 1961
A fresh and crisp wine from the Mosel, very typical of its kind. The 1961 vintage on the Mosel was most successful, and the wines have the characteristic 'snap' that one associates with the district which also produces ideal summer wines.   11/3

CUVÉE DU LION CHAMPAGNE
Our own brands of Champagne are selected with the greatest care and compare most favourably with the better known and more expensive non-vintage 'Grand Marque'.   22/3

AN APERITIF FOR JUNE

If you are in France this summer and ask for 'un Kir' you should be given an aperitif named after Canon Kir of Dijon, a drink perhaps more commonly known as 'un Vin Blanc Cassis'.

Into a large wine glass pour a dash of sirop de Cassis and top up with ice cold, dry, White Burgundy. The amount of Cassis – Syrup of Blackcurrants – that you use must depend upon individual taste. Top up with soda for a long drink.

MONTAGNY, Dry White Burgundy   10/3
SIROP DE CASSIS   11/6
June 1964

Sir Francis Chichester

MAN OF DEVON

I am not really a yachtsman, I am a navigator.
SIR FRANCIS CHICHESTER
Oh England! model to thy inward greatness,
Like little body with a mighty heart.
SHAKESPEARE, *Henry V* – Chorus Act II

It is curious, how the hidden depth of memory can be revived by one incident and then embrace so many people, places and events in one's life. It must be fifteen years since I trod on a large lump of oil concealed by the sand of one of my favourite beaches, which lies just below the second tee of Thurlestone Golf Club, and was the helpless spectator of a sea bird – a guillemot, if I remember rightly – blinded by oil, circling on the surface of the sea.

These memories came flooding back with the wreck of the *Torrey Canyon* and my deep sympathy goes out to all those whose beaches and livelihood have been afflicted by the cruel and filthy pollution from her cargo. At the time of this tragic disaster, The Duke of Edinburgh unveiled, in Trafalgar Square on 2nd April, the bust of Admiral of the Fleet, Lord Cunningham of Hyndhope, to stand in the glorious company of Nelson, Jellicoe and Beatty. This reminded me that it was almost exactly twenty-six years ago that I crossed the sea from Alexandria to Piraeus in one of his ships: HMS *Gloucester*.

Cunningham, a great patriot and a fighting admiral, reminds us in his book *A Sailor's Odyssey* that Britain is self-supporting neither in food, oil, nor raw materials, and that our very birthright is to be a maritime nation. He would have seen a warning in the *Torrey Canyon* disaster, a reminder that our livelihood and life alike depend on the sea, and that the navy should continue its part in the defence of our kingdom. We should never forget his message after our crippling losses off Crete, in 1941, including so many of the gallant ship's company of HMS *Gloucester*: 'It takes the navy three years to build a ship; it would take three hundred to build a tradition.'

So, as I write on St George's Day, my mind turns to Plymouth where I would give much to be standing on The Hoe on that day in May, when Sir Francis Chichester completes his epic voyage. Looking through my newspaper cuttings I find this entry on 26th October 1966: 'Fifty-eight days out of Plymouth and I've sailed 8,150 miles and the distance to Sydney in now 5,750'. Francis Chichester still had 20,000 miles ahead to complete his voyage to Plymouth, alone and at the age of sixty-five. What a man! Of one thing I am sure; the spirit of Francis Drake and Andrew Cunningham will be there to greet and salute this navigator and man of courage.

June 1967

Ave atque Vale

On their own merits modest men are dumb.
GEORGE COLMAN, 1762–1836. *Heir at Law*
The applause of the crowd makes the head giddy, but the attestation of a reasonable man makes the heart glad
SIR RICHARD STEELE, 1672–1729. *The Spectator*

Once upon a time there were modest and devoted students of wine who, over a period of a hundred years and more, spread abroad, by their loving care and appreciation, the reputation for quality of certain wines. These wines became famous names amongst their friends throughout the world of wine lovers. Today, without a tear of regret or a sigh of gratitude, the greedy custodians of these illustrious names cry 'Demand Exceeds Supply', as they set new heights for the price of their wines. '*Ave atque Vale*' we reply in sorrow and amazement, and wonder for how long the hard won reputation of their names will be perpetuated in the hands of the few buyers and consumers who can afford to pay their prices.

Be that as it may, in Alsace the wines are named by the grape variety, such as Riesling, Sylvaner, or Traminer, and not by the names of estates or châteaux. It is, however, the name of the grower, which, above all guarantees their quality – and I know a man of Alsace, who is not only modest but whose head has not yet been made giddy by the applause of the crowd. His name is Jean Hugel. Since 1639, and during eleven consecutive genera-tions, the great and noble tradition of wine growing has been

88

passed from father to son. If Jean Hugel sacrifices quality for quantity, or prices his wines out of the world market, may I be struck dumb!

I could write pages of attestation to the courage and patience of the Alsatians in overcoming the ravages of two world wars, let alone the forty-eight years of occupation by the Germans, when they were forced to sacrifice quality for the quantity of common blend wines. Since 1919 the battle for quality has been won and their wines justify the faith that Christopher's have always placed in them. They remain, with few exceptions, my favourite white wines.

It was after an evening of good food, wine and music with Jean Hugel, when we listened to Schubert's 'Trout' Quintet, that I remembered another man who deserves our applause as much as the great singers he has 'accompanied' with such artistry, insight and sympathy. So I dedicate my 'Alsatian' Quintet to Jean Hugel, wine grower, and to Gerald Moore, pianist, both of them modest and great artists in their own right, and to whom I express my gratitude for the pleasure they have given me.

FOOTNOTE   At the time of writing, 25th April 1966, the price of one hogshead of Ch. Lafite 1964 (48 gallons) still holds a substantial lead over the price of £554 for one ton of Zambian Copper!

FOOTNOTE FOOTNOTE   In 1970 the price for the 1969 vintage has broken the 'sound barrier' of over £1,000 for one hogshead!

Colour prejudice

Communication – *'the imparting, conveying or exchange of ideas, knowledge etc (whether by speech, writing or signs)'. 1690.*
OXFORD ENGLISH DICTIONARY

We are all so busy that most of us, myself included, neglect one of the decencies of life – communication; and possibly the failure of society is the failure of communication. Unless we are born blind, colour also plays a very important part in our lives, whether it be the yellow of daffodils at Easter, the ruby of wine or the colour of our skins.

Thus it was that the colour of a medal ribbon led me to a failure in communication, on an evening when the escalator at Waterloo had broken down and brought me, in a shuffllng queue, inching my way up to a Police Constable with a row of medal ribbons on his chest. 'What's that medal?' I asked, pointing to the first one. 'North West Frontier India, Sir,' he replied. 'When were you in India?' '1930, Sir.' 'That was the year I left India. You look much too young to have been in India in 1930,' I retorted. 'Well Sir, I ran away from home to join the Army when I was sixteen.' 'Good luck to you!' I said, as I began my long climb. As I reached the top, a brown-skinned man spoke to me. 'I couldn't help overhearing what you said to the policeman. I was born in India in 1930.' 'Good heavens'! What a coincidence!' I said. 'I had a wonderful time in your country and shall never forget it.' We shook hands, and in that instant of time he was my brother in human society. But only for that fleeting second, because in the rush hour at Waterloo Station he quickly disappeared. Too late I cursed myself for failing to ask him for his name and address, so that I could preserve and enlarge such a precious encounter. It was a bitter failure in communication. To find and communicate with my policeman was easy: there are not many blue uniformed holders of that particular coloured medal ribbon! My thanks to the British Transport Police for arranging another meeting.

Politics and colour prejudice apart (they form no part of these leaflets), and leaving out champagne for the moment, all table wines are basically red or white, and depend for their colour on the skins of the grapes from which they are made – black or white. However, there is the 'half-caste', the pale red wine which we call rosé, known under its humbler and older name as 'Vin Gris', and which used to be made generally from a marriage of black and white grapes. The modern method is more refined, usually using black grapes from locally deemed 'noble vines' – except that the moment the must has acquired the desired tint it is drawn off from the black grape skins. Whether as men we swear allegiance to red wines or as women to white wines, we cannot deny the 'opinion polls' which tell us that both sexes drink vast quantities of rosé wines believing them to combine the more attractive qualities of each in a 'robe' more beautiful than either.

CH. DE TRINQUEVEDEL, TAVEL, 1966   23/–
ROSÉ DE GRENACHE, DOMAINE PATERNEL,
CASSIS, 1964   27/–
ROSÉ DE BANDOL, DOMAINE TEMPIER
BANDOL, 1966   28/–
CH. DE SELLE, DOMAINE OTT, PROVENCE, 1966   29/6
June 1968

Champagne and ballooning are synonymous

'Get in,' I was ordered. 'Get those bottles,' I shouted to a by-stander, pointing at the two Maison Christophe lying in the shade of a car. As I clambered into the balloon basket, squeezing in beside the other four people, I was handed the two precious bottles. It was impossible to do other than clutch them, for we were already standing on a layer of sandbags (mostly filled by beginner-me), and five people in a wicker basket roughly four feet by three is a little intimate!

It was my first flight. I had the good fortune not only to be in Anthony Smith's 'Jambo' (she burst into flames the following weekend) but to have Charles Dollfus, the world's leading aeronaut, as pilot. Minutes later the last command of 'Hands off' came, and we gently lifted into the clear July sky. I managed to push one bottle down by my feet and found myself wondering how high we would have to go before the top of the bottle blew off! Always one for safety I started twisting off the wire and then thumbed the cork gently while Jean Lesqui, the other Frenchman, held a rather mangled plastic cup I had in my pocket. Approval from Jean and Charles when I eased out the cork with no vulgar pop; and though we all tried drinking from the bottle, it was very difficult and chin dribbling, so we had to resort to sharing the cup. No champagne has ever, ever, ever tasted so good as that shared bottle under the vast orange and silver curve of 'Jambo'.

By this time we had started to float over the edge of the fens and were about 1000 feet up. Since you travel with the wind, balloon-ing is absolutely silent, and from several hundred feet above them you can hear clearly dogs barking and people shouting messages to you. We had travelled for forty minutes when, seeing an empty stretch of fens ahead with no road (for the pick-up team), Charles cut the trail rope to slow our progress. 'Hands in,' the photographer and I – both first-flighters – were told, and the ground rushed up to meet us at an alarming speed.

The most bone-shattering thump and we landed – tipped a bit, dragged a bit, but landed the right way up. At best a balloon landing is a 'controlled accident' – but this, compared with a subsequent one I made, was armchair-ease. We stayed in until the balloon was deflated (27 cubic feet of hydrogen). Then we climbed out and began the business of folding it all up.

Silently I handed the remaining (well-shaken!) bottle of Masion Christophe to Jean. He opened it and poured – not too much – over my hair so that it trickled down my forehead and nose – only a little finding its way into my mouth. Then a good handful of sand followed it over my head – my first flight balloon christening was over.

We marked our landing by drowning the two empty bottles in a deep dyke. Future archaeologists take note.

ANNE LEWIS-SMITH

June 1969

The Tiffin Basket

English military gentlemen are traditionally fond of their wine and food, and often uncommonly well informed about cookery and the management of the kitchen. Several regular army officers have written successful cookery books. Among the better known are Colonel Kenney Herbert's *Culinary Jottings for Madras* (1886) – an indispensable book for curry addicts – and his *Commonsense Cookery*, written after his retirement, when he opened a cookery school in Sloane Street.

The late Sir Francis Colchester-Wemyss, in common with Colonel Kenney Herbert, had served in India (indeed it would have been difficult in those days for a professional soldier to avoid doing so) and in *The Pleasures of the Table* (1931, reprinted 1962)[1] hints that his interest in cookery was a by-product of army life in British India. An early necessity to come to grips with the recipes, which, as mess secretary, he attempted to transmit to his regiment's Hindustani cooks, fostered a natural interest in food and wine.

Similarly unexpected beginnings may well have been responsible for a whole school of cookery-writers, whose books would make an entertaining and uniquely English collection (in France it is doctors and engineers who are the great amateurs of cookery writing), in which would certainly figure the works of Major L . . . author of *The Pytchley Cookery Book* (1886), and *Breakfasts, Luncheons and Ball Suppers* (1887). Both these books contain diverting dissertations on racing, shooting, and travelling luncheons.

Major L . . .'s luncheon basket, which he himself designed with the assistance of Messrs Farrow and Jackson (the firm still famous for the supply of wine bins and cellar fitments), played an important part in the major's life. Among other sensible innovations, the basket was designed to hold a pint bottle of champagne or claret, and one of sherry or Salutaris water. As he observes, 'in the summer, the dust and heat make one thirsty, hot and uncomfortable. A good lunch and a glass of good champagne assist to while away the tediousness of the journey, oil the wheels of life, and improve the temper'.

[1] James Nisbet and Co., Digswell Place, Welwyn, Herts.

Whether, in the dust and heat, the major contrived to get his champagne and his Salutaris water cooled to a suitable temperature he does not relate (our grandfathers, forever on the march with their champagne and travelling provisions, would have appreciated today's insulated picnic bags). But he goes into some detail as to the solid content of the luncheon basket. It was to include, among other trifles, beefsteak or chicken pie, fillets of chicken, grouse or pheasant, cold stewed beef, lamb cutlets in aspic, slices of galantine, lemon biscuits, cakes of all sorts, mince pies and plum pudding. Inclusion of that last item betrays Major L . . .'s Indian service days. Colonel Kenney Herbert also recommended that 'a nice piece of brisket of beef, trimmed into a neat shape, is a very handy thing for the tiffin basket – and a really good cold plum pudding, in which a glass of brandy has been included'.

They were right about the plum pudding, those Victorian officers. It does make a marvellous travelling and picnic dish, and is rather more welcome in the open air than ever it is on the Christmas table. As for the pressed brisket of beef, one of the best of English cold dishes, whether for indoors or out, here is a simple recipe:

PRESSED BRISKET OF BEEF

A 5–6 lb. piece of salt brisket should be soaked in water for a couple of hours before cooking. Put it in a deep oven dish with two or three carrots, a sliced onion, a dozen peppercorns, a couple of bayleaves, and fresh water to cover. Cook, closely covered, in the centre of a very moderate oven, gas No. 2–3, 330°F, for three to four hours, until the meat is very tender but not falling to pieces.

Take the joint from the liquid (which will make the basis of a good beetroot consommé or onion soup), wrap it in greaseproof paper, put it between two boards or dishes with a 4–7 lb. weight on the top. Leave until next day before trimming and cutting.

AVOCADO SALAD

For indoor eating, this is the salad advocated by Sir Francis Colchester-Wemyss as making the ideal combination with cold

94

pressed beef. 'Make an ordinary well-seasoned oil and vinegar dressing, pour a dessertspoonful or so into the middle of each half, and then with a teaspoon detach the flesh in small pieces till nothing but the thick skin is left, and the flesh is all in the centre. Mix this well with the dressing, and serve, as it is, in the skin.'

COLD CHICKEN VERONICA

Many years ago, when I was living in a tropical climate, I evolved this recipe to replace chicken mayonnaise for picnics and cold suppers. Prepared ahead of time, which they should be, dishes of chicken or fish and mayonnaise tend to acquire an oily and unappetizing appearance in warm weather, and especially after a long car journey. No matter what the circumstances or the temperature, the cream sauce in this Chicken Veronica retains all its pristine qualities for many hours.

A day or two in advance cook a nice fat boiling fowl of about 4 lb. weight, with its giblets (but not the liver, keep that for an omelette, or as a *bonne bouche* for the cat) with four or five carrots, a couple of onions, a piece of celery, a clove of garlic, a faggot of parsley stalks, tarragon and a strip of lemon peel, 2 tablespoonfuls of salt and water to cover.

The chicken will need about 2½ to 3 hours very gentle simmering. Keep the pot covered but tilt the lid to allow the steam to escape. Should it be more convenient the cooking can be done in a very slow oven. When the chicken is tender and the flesh beginning to come away from the drumsticks, take it out of the pot and leave it to cool. Strain the stock, measure off a quarter pint for the sauce, and keep the rest aside for a soup or for further cooking with fresh beef and shin of veal for a double consommé. Other ingredients for the sauce are: ½ pint of double cream, 4 tablespoonfuls of rich sherry or madeira and the yolks of four eggs.

Put the cream, the ¼ pint of chicken stock and the sherry into a wide and shallow saucepan such as a sauté pan. When this mixture is hot, pour a little of it on to the very well whisked egg yolks. Stir thoroughly. Return all to the first pan. Stir over very gentle heat until the sauce begins to thicken. In a wide pan this happens quite quickly, in a tall deep one it takes an eternity.

95

But don't let the mixture overheat, and keep stirring all the time or the eggs will scramble. The finished sauce should be of the consistency of a home-made custard. Rectify the seasoning. You may need more salt, possibly lemon juice. You may even add a drop or two of armagnac, cognac or calvados, or perhaps a little more sherry. When you take the sauce from the heat, go on stirring it until it has cooled a little.

Carve the chicken into nice, even-sized pieces, not too big and not too small. Keep all skin and bone for strengthening the original stock when you cook it up again.

Arrange the chicken pieces in a shallow dish. Pour the sauce through a strainer over them. If it looks rather liquid at this stage remember that it thickens as it cools.

Before serving, sprinkle chopped parsley, tarragon or chives over the dish.

At Christmas time this recipe can be usefully applied to cold turkey.

RICE SALAD

This makes just the right accompaniment to the chicken veronica. For six to eight people: Cook 1 lb. of good quality rice in a gallon-and-half capacity saucepan nearly full of boiling salted water. Add half a lemon, and when the water comes back to the boil float a couple of tablespoonfuls of olive oil on the top. This will help prevent the water boiling over. The rice will be cooked in twelve to eighteen minutes depending upon the type of rice you are using. In any case, keep it on the firm side.

As soon as you have drained the rice in a colander turn it into a big bowl. Immediately, add any necessary salt, approximately 6 tablespoonfuls of olive oil, 2 teaspoonfuls of tarragon vinegar, two shallots sliced into paper-thin rounds, and a good quantity of grated nutmeg. This latter seasoning makes the whole difference.

Have ready a cucumber, peeled, sliced in four lengthways, the seeds removed, the flesh cut into small cubes, and seasoned with salt. Mix these with the rice. Add also, if you like, a dozen or so stoned black olives, a few cubes of raw celery, and a few shreds of raw green sweet pepper (tinned red peppers are not to be recommended for this dish, they are too soft, too sweet, and too obtrusive). Mix all together very lightly and the salad is ready, except for a sprinkling of chives or parsley.

In the winter when cucumber is unobtainable try instead little cubes of green or yellow honey-dew melon which goes well with both chicken and turkey.

ELIZABETH DAVID

A Dinner in June

Alsace is often called 'le pays du bien vivre' and it is certainly a world-famous gastronomical region where are to be found all sorts of freshwater fish, home-cured hams, a large variety of pâtés, a wide choice of game, as well as the domestic pig and chicken and in particular the goose. You will also find a regiment of sausages, sweet dishes, cakes, biscuits, tarts and flans.

Christopher's wines prompt thought of goose liver pâté and sweet hams, or, as I've chosen, river trout and the local tarte à l'oignon, a variation of the classic quiche from neighbouring Lorraine. For dessert, our own early summer markets should provide as good as the orchards of Alsace.

Here, then is an Alsatian dinner to match our Vins d'Alsace:

ONION TART

For six people: ½ lb. flaky or shortcrust pastry, 1 lb. finely sliced onions, three rashers bacon, 2½ oz. butter, 1½ oz. flour, 1½ gills milk, two eggs, seasoning. Line the pastry into an 8 inch flan ring. Prick the base. Melt the butter, add the sliced onions, and diced bacon, and cook gently for fifteen minutes without allowing the onions to brown. Remove the pan from the heat and stir in the flour. Add the milk and eggs beaten together. Season the mixture and carefully pour it into the flan case. Bake at gas No. 6, 400°F for twenty-five to thirty minutes.

TROUT WITH ALMONDS

For six people: six trout, 3 oz. butter, lemon juice, seasoned flour, blanched split almonds, chopped parsley slices of lemon.

Wash and dry the cleaned trout and roll them in the seasoned flour. Melt the butter in a frying pan and when it is foaming, lay in the fish. Fry gently until one side is brown, then turn carefully and brown the second side. Lift out and put on a serving dish. Keep warm. Put the almonds into the pan, with a little more butter if necessary, add a squeeze of lemon and fry quickly until just brown. Pour the hot butter and the almonds over the fish, and garnish with slices of lemon dipped in chopped parsley. Serve with English new potatoes.

As vegetables are not really acceptable with trout, a good mixed salad containing cooked peas, beans and asparagus can be served as a separate course after the fish, or even after the Onion Tart.

PEACHES CARDINAL

For six people: six fresh peaches (preferably white), 1 lb. raspberries, icing sugar.

Sieve the raspberries and sweeten with the icing sugar. Skin the peaches but leave them whole. Put them in a glass dish, pour the raspberry purée over them and serve with cream.

PRUDENCE LEITH

No Alsatian meal is complete without one of their famous FRUIT BRANDIES! They must be drunk from glasses which have been previously iced – cold has the effect of bringing out the flavour of the fruit.

MIRABELLE – golden plum   80/–

THE HUGEL QUINTET, OPUS 1964

SPOREN   19/7

A blend of Riesling and Traminer, combining delicacy and body, from the famous vineyards of Sporen.

RIESLING GRAND CRU   20/6

Dry with exquisite flavour, distinguished bouquet and great breeding, especially suitable with white fish.

TRAMINER GRAND CRU   22/9
Deep, rich, lingering flavour and pronounced bouquet, can be
drunk throughout the meal.
GEWURZTRAMINER GRAND CRU   23/9
Gewurz means spicy, thus a Traminer with a very pronounced
distinct bouquet and flavour.
MUSCAT RESERVE EXCEPTIONELLE   26/3
This is the finest dry Muscat, superb dry fruity flavour and
bouquet of the Muscat grape.
June 1966

In the Grand Manner

In June, Mr Borra, the head chef at Quaglino's, is going to cook
Coulibiac of Salmon for my Regimental Dinner. How he makes
this delicious dish for a hundred people is a mystery to me, but I
do know that he is a great chef. So I asked him to give his recipe
for six people, and here it is.

'Have ready 2 lb. of puff pastry. Stiffen in butter $1\frac{1}{2}$ lb. of fresh
salmon collops (no skin or bones). Prepare $\frac{1}{4}$ lb. mushrooms and
one large chopped onion and fry them in butter. Cook $\frac{1}{2}$ lb. rice in
consommé, two hard boiled eggs chopped, and 1 lb. of vesiga
roughly chopped and cooked either in consommé or salted water.

'Vesiga is the spine marrow of a sturgeon. For this weight of
cooked vesiga about $2\frac{1}{4}$ oz. should be needed. It should be
soaked for twelve hours in cold water and then cooked for about
three hours – then cooled. This is an expensive matter and is only
bought by the yard; but Quaglino's are willing to supply it in
small quantities.

'Roll the puff pastry into a 12 inch $\times$ 8 inch rectangle and
spread, in successive layers, the rice, the collops of salmon, the
chopped vesiga the mushrooms and the onion, finishing with a
layer of rice. Moisten the edges of the pastry and draw the longest
ends towards each other over the layers of garnish and join them.
Now fold the other two ends over to the centre. Place the coulibiac
on a baking tray with the joined ends underneath, and leave in the
fridge for twenty-five minutes. Make a slit in the top and bake in a
moderate oven for forty-five to fifty minutes. Fill the coulibiac

with freshly melted butter when you withdraw it from the oven, slice and serve immediately with a sauce Bercy. This is a reduction in white wine of shallots, ordinary white sauce (made after reducing) and chopped parsley put in at the last minute.'

This princely dish deserves a full-bodied dry white wine, and I know none better for bouquet and flavour than the wines of my old friend Jean Hugel.

More Summer Dishes

SARDINE AND LEMON PATÉ

Here is an inexpensive starter for a summer meal, easily and quickly made, and delicious with a glass of cold dry sherry.

For six people; Take two tins of sardines (Marie Elizabeth), 4 oz. of butter, the juice of one lemon, plenty of ground black pepper, a little salt and a teaspoonful of made mustard Dijon or Florida. Beat all together until smooth and put into the fridge. Spoon into little dishes, garnish with parsley and serve with hot toast and a glass of well chilled dry sherry.

The increasing popularity of the use of herbs is one of the best things that has happened to British home cooking for many years. If you are not yet converted, try the following recipes. The herbs should be fresh and chopped only a few moments before use for best results, but at a pinch the dried variety will do.

TUNNY FISH SALAD

Break up the contents of a tin of tunny fish into small pieces, season with wine vinegar and a little French mustard. Add equal quantities of raw celery and tinned pineapple cut into small pieces and a generous pinch or two of tarragon. Mix well and pile in little heaps on crisp lettuce leaves, then chill. Sprinkle with chopped chives before serving.

LAMB CUTLETS PROVENCE STYLE

Take a boned best end of neck and rub the inside with a cut clove of garlic. Sprinkle with pepper and salt and then roll up Swiss roll fashion. Cut into eight cutlets and secure each one with a wooden cocktail stick. Arrange these in a large frying pan with a little olive oil and brown them lightly on each side. Add a large onion cut in slices and continue to fry until the onion is soft. Add six or eight skinned tomatoes, one green pepper depipped and cut into slices, a dessertspoonful of tomato purée, ¼ pint of dry white wine and ½ pint or so of stock (or water with a bouillon cube). Allow the whole thing to simmer gently for about ten minutes, then add a small handful of rosemary and continue the simmering process for fifteen minutes or so, until the sauce has thickened.

Arrange the cutlets on a serving dish, surround with the tomatoes and other vegetables and pour the rest of the sauce over. Lots of freshly chopped parsley on top just before it goes to the table adds as much to the flavour as to the wonderfully appetising appearance of this dish.

LORRAINE CREAMS

Everybody has heard of the Lorraine Quiche, but you may find this an interesting little savoury based on the same idea.

Grill three rashers of streaky bacon until they are so crisp that they will break into small pieces. Take 3 oz. grated cheese, Gruyère and Parmesan mixed are best, but one can make do with others. Stir the cheese into ¼ pint of cream and then stir in one very well beaten egg, the bits of bacon and a dash of salt and pepper. Stir once again and then put the mixture in little individual ovenproof dishes and cook in a pretty hot oven. These creams are not soufflés but nearly so and will rise a little, turning a nice golden colour.

LESLIE HOARE

ICED SHRIMP SOUP

I find this delicately flavoured soup simple to make and delicious for a hot June day. Prawns may be used instead of shrimps, and it can be prepared the day before.

One pint cooked shrimps, 3 tablespoonfuls white breadcrumbs, 1½ pints of fish stock made from the shells of the shrimps, a small piece (about ½ lb.) of any white fish, one onion, lemon peel, herbs, salt and pepper, 1 teacupful cream or milk, one egg yolk, a pinch of nutmeg, the juice of half a lemon, cucumber, fennel or watercress.

Prepare the stock by simmering the fish and the shrimp shells, the onion, herbs and lemon peel in 1½ pints of water for about twenty minutes. Strain it and put into it the white breadcrumbs. Reserving a few shrimps for the garnish, pound the rest in a mortar adding the lemon juice and nutmeg. Add gradually the stock and the breadcrumbs until the mixture is creamy. Heat up in a pan for five minutes and then press through a wire sieve.

Beat the egg yolk and the cream or milk together, stir in 2 or 3 tablespoonfuls of the hot soup, return the mixture to the pan and stir until hot, but don't let it boil. When cooked add about an inch of peeled cucumber diced small, a little chopped fennel or watercress and the reserved shrimps. Serve very well iced and garnished with a slice of lemon.

French Country Cooking

Champagne

WHAT'S IN A NAME?

CECIL GRAHAM : What is a cynic?
LORD DARLINGTON : A man who knows the price of everything and the value of nothing.
OSCAR WILDE: *Lady Windermere's Fan.*

The tendency today is to drink champagne as an aperitif. I can think of no better way to revive the one-time fashion of drinking champagne with a meal than to open a bottle of Bollinger R.D. 1955 with Elizabeth David's cold chicken veronica – or indeed a bottle of any of the wines mentioned below.

'What goes up seldom, if ever, comes down' is a saying which all Wine Merchants know only too well when they come to collect for the Exchequer the duty on a bottle of champagne.

What a pity there was no room to squeeze the Chancellor of the Exchequer into the basket of the balloon 'Jambo', so that he might have seen for himself that what goes up can come down, even if only by a controlled accident. Alas! On the 15th April 1969 the duty on a bottle of our Maison Christophe champagne soared to 7s. 5½d.

A few days later my wife and I were sitting in Elizabeth David's kitchen, the occasion for which was to taste her home baked English loaf, together with an Edwardian sausage and, wondrous to relate, to wash it down with a glass of superb champagne – Louis Roederer Cristal 1962. The price of the bread and sausages, the value of the wine – who knows? But the combination was memorable for its simplicity and quality, and typical of our hostess.

In recent years the leading Champagne houses have added a special marque of wine to their normal 'vintage' and 'non-vintage' brands. These wines, made up from their finest cuvées, are the ultimate in the skill of the producer, and each bears the individualistic style of its house. Like Oscar Wilde's cynic, I do know their price – they are expensive! But their value I leave to your palate, which I am confident will give a verdict to justify your extravagance.

The list is by no means complete, nor are the wines placed in order – but they are all in the top ten!

CRISTAL, brut 1962 Louis Roederer	69/6
AVIZE, blanc de blancs 1962 Pommery & Greno	63/6
DOM PERIGNON, 1961 Moët & Chandon	72/9
RÉSERVE DE L'EMPEREUR, blanc de blancs 1961 Mercier	68/3
PRINCE A. DE BOURBON PARME, brut 1961	80/–
BOLLINGER R. D.[1], 1955	70/6

The Baking of an English Loaf by ELIZABETH DAVID, 2s. 6d.
The Edwardian Sausage is not to be missed. For full particulars of this and other products, write or telephone to Natural Farms Foods, 9 St Loo Mansions, Cheyne Gardens, London, SW3. Tel. 01–352 9058.
June 1969

[1] R. D. stands for 'recently disgorged', and this wine was not disgorged until January 1968 – thus giving a youthful freshness to an already mellow and mature wine.

A Wine Lover's Code

To become a wine lover you must, first and foremost, realize that you have a palate, a precious gift given to you by nature. At the onset of your wine-drinking days it may be good, bad or indifferent, and it will certainly be uneducated. But by constant effort, research, reading and tasting it can be improved out of all recognition to give you a hobby which will bring you unlimited scope and enjoyment. Take courage! I know scores of wine lovers outside the Wine Trade who are just as good or better judges and tasters of wine as their professional brothers; their only handicap is the lack of opportunity to taste and taste again, and the cost of such tastings.

Here is a Code for Wine Lovers, many of the rules of which I have, regretably, broken from time to time.

Approach your tasting of any wine with humility, or you may be riding for a fall.

Whenever possible taste 'blind'. You will avoid prejudice, and profit from your mistakes, when you eventually know what you have tasted.

Judge all wines on their merits: do not be seduced by their names and reputations.

Be critical, without being dogmatic or pompous.

Be fearless in your own opinions, and respect the opinions of others.

Listen to everyone for information that will improve your knowledge of wine. It is surprising the invaluable tips you can pick up.

Keep notes of the wines you taste. This will stand you in good stead and aid your 'taste memory'.

Read all the books on wine on which you can lay your hands.

Avoid name dropping – no one is impressed.

Avoid making others appear ignorant by your superior knowledge.

Do not be disappointed if your friends fail to make any comment on your best bottle of wine.

Be tolerant of other peoples' palates. We all have different tastes in wine and food.

Avoid embarrassing and boring your friends with guessing games, unless you know that they genuinely enjoy such distractions from the appreciation of the wine you are giving them.

Join Wine Societies or suchlike tasting circles, and in particular the International Wine and Food Society, the best of them all.

Make a friend of your Wine Merchant and shop around from several of them.

Beware of becoming a dilettante or a wine bore.

Last, but by no means least, never lose your sense of humour about wine, nor take your hobby and yourself too seriously. Wine is not an academic lesson. It is pure joy to be shared with your friends.

Here are two recent books which I think will appeal and be of help to wine lovers:
Wine Tasting by MICHAEL BROADBENT.
Wine Lovers' Handbook by PAMELA VANDYKE PRICE.

July

At 5 o'clock we all went down to the beach leaving
Mrs. Cowper Coles in her Bath Chair on the top of
the Cliff. Mrs. Powles, Miss Deason, Gussie and
Alice sat down by the bathing machine to sketch
Sampson's Cottage at the mouth of the Chine.
Minna, Sherard, Commerell, Cowper Todd and I
set to work to dig sand castles and trenches. The
tide was going out, a number of children were
paddling in the shallow water left by the white
retreating surges, and it was a fair sight to watch
the merry girls with their pretty white feet and
bare limbs wading through the little rippling waves
or walking on the wet and shining sand.

FRANCIS KILVERT 1875

Blue plaques

The residences of the ornaments of their history cannot but be precious to all thinking Englishmen.

WILLIAM EWART, 1798–1869

'Paddington-Exeter-Plymouth and Penzance. Plymouth first stop.' was a cry which never failed to thrill me when I caught the Cornish Riviera Express (dep. Paddington 10.30 am; arr. Exeter 1.30 pm), to return home from school. First, the solemn ritual of inspecting the engine, hoping it would be *King George V*, and then back to the rear coaches to lean out and watch for the light to turn green on the stroke of 10.30, and thrill to the guard's shrill whistle. Three hours later, to the minute, I would lean out of the window to watch the Exeter coach being slipped and glide into the station while the rest of the train steamed on to 'Plymouth, first stop!'

Little did I imagine that many years later I would have, as a partner in Christopher's, a man whose ancestor was the architect of this famous Great Western Railroad. Curiously enough, my partner lives in Chelsea, and so does the blue plaque of his ancestor Brunel which adorns No. 98 Cheyne Walk. 'Brunel – Sir Marc Isambard, 1769–1849, and Isambard Kingdom Brunel, 1806–59, Civil Engineers, lived here.' For the record, there are five plaques in Cheyne Walk: Brunel, No. 98, Mrs Gaskell, No. 93, Rosetti, No. 16, Whistler, No. 96, and 'George Eliot', No. 4. Quite a collection! No other street can boast of such a number and such illustrious names.

However, I live in Westminster and we have seventy-one plaques to a mere nineteen in Chelsea! In the morning, when I walk to our shop (we are tradesmen and proud of it), I can salute Sir Francis Galton, founder of eugenics, at No. 42 Rutland Gate. After that I go by way of Gainsborough – 82 Pall Mall, and bow my head to William Pitt, Earl of Chatham, Edward Geoffrey Stanley, Earl of Derby and William Ewart Gladstone, all of No. 10 St James's Square, and then safely round the corner into Jermyn Street with a thought for Sir Isaac Newton at No. 87.

A small diversion will take me past Napoleon III at 1c King Street, and I have only to walk to our cellars to take in my stride such great men as Thomas Sheraton at 163 Wardour Street,

Edmund Burke at 37 Gerrard Street, and John Dryden, with memories of Mrs Meyrick's famous night-club of the twenties, at No. 43.

White Burgundies of exceptional quality are scarce and hard to find, let alone white Rhône wines, and I now wish to award a special plaque to four wines and their growers because of their undoubted excellence.

BLUE PLAQUE AWARDS

To Fernand Morey for his	
CHASSAGNE MONTRACHET, 1962	31/6
To Marc Morey for his	
CHASSAGNE MONTRACHET, 1961	34/6
To Bouchard Père et Fils for their	
BIENVENUES-BATARD-MONTRACHET, 1962	48/6
To Paul Jaboulet for his	
HERMITAGE, LE CHEVALIER DE STERIMBERG, 1964	21/6

July 1966

Cures for chattering teeth

July used to be accented on the first syllable and as late as 1798 Wordsworth wrote

> *In March, December, and in July*
> *' Tis all the same with Harry Gill;*
> *The neighbours tell, and tell you truly,*
> *His teeth they chatter, chatter still.*

WINE CUPS

July is the ideal month for a Wine Cup when so many fruits are in season, and H. Warner Allen gives us some basic rules for its success.

The first step in mixing must be to lay the fruit, sliced, if it be not soft, at the bottom of the bowl or jug. Do not add too much sugar; a lack of sweetness can be corrected later by a touch of liqueur. Add a glass or two of brandy to the fruit, and allow to stand for a quarter of an hour before adding the wine.

The ideal blend is one bottle of sparkling wine to every two or three bottles of still wine; if no sparkling is available soda-water must be added. The ingredients must be thoroughly stirred and controlled by repeated tasting. Restraint in sugaring leaves room for a touch of Maraschino or Orange Curacao. The refrigerator may make ice unnecessary[1], but if ice is used allow plenty of time for its dilution. Slices of lemon, sprigs of bergamot or lemon mint may be added, and borage is much more satisfactory than the customary cucumber peel.

Here is another recipe for a cup, from no less a person than Professor George Saintsbury, and one which is hard to beat. I quote from the great man's own words.

'I once invented one which was extremely popular, and had a curious history later. Instead of soda-water I used sparkling Moselle, in the proportion of a pint of this to a bottle of Claret, with thick slices of pineapple instead of lemon, and one lump of ice as big as a baby's head. It was astonishing how the people lapped it up, and nobody complained next day (I gave it at an evening party) of headache, though some ladies did say: "wasn't that delicious cup of yours rather strong? I slept so soundly after it."'

From *The Gourmet's Companion*, Eyre & Spottiswoode.

Sir Kenelm Digby's fancies

Often quoted as an example of the dear quaint rules by which our ancestors cooked – a sauce to be stirred 'An Ava Maria while' – a soup to be 'boil'd simpringly' – the posthumously published *Closet of the Eminently learned Sir Kenelm Digby Kt. Opened, Published with his Son's Consent 1669*[2] has been in other respects underestimated. The book is a beautiful piece of English kitchen literature as well as a collection of recipes set down with considerable accuracy, and of great historical interest.

[1] You can obtain delivery of ice in the London area by telephoning, the day before your party, to United Carlo Gatti. 01-228 0072. (10 lb. bags in cubes at 6s. od. per bag).
[2] Reprinted in 1910, with introductory notes and glossary by Anne Macdonell.

It was Sir Kenelm's evident mania for the brewing of mead, metheglin, hydromel and suchlike popular drinks of the Stuart period that was the undoing of his reputation as a cookery author. As arranged for publication (possibly by a man who had been his steward), the book opens with upwards of one hundred recipes for Digby's favourite brews, based on honey or home-made ale, highly spiced and flavoured with all the herbs and flowers of seventeenth-century English gardens and hedgerows. The instructions and lists of ingredients are repetitive and few readers persevere beyond the first half-dozen recipes. Were the forbidding blocks of print divided up, as they can be without in the slightest respect altering the punctuation or the flow, into verse form, it would be seen that, like all the best recipes, these are runes, litanies, almost even magic spells. They should be read aloud:

TO MAKE WHITE METHEGLIN

Take Sweet marjoram, sweet-bryar-buds,
Violet leaves, strawberry leaves,
Of each one handful,
And a good handful of Violet-flowers
(The dubble ones are the best)
Broad Thyme, Borrage, Agrimony,
Of each half a handful,
And two or three branches of Rosemary,

The seeds of Carvi[1], Coriander, and Fennel,
Of each two spoonfuls,
And three or four blades of large-mace.
Boil all these in eight Gallons of running-water,
Three quarters of an hour.

Then strain it, and when it is but blood-warm,
Put in as much of the best honey
As will make the Liquor
Bear an egg the breadth of sixpence above the water.
Then boil it again as long as any scum will rise.
Then set it abroad a cooling;
And when it is almost cold,
Put in a half a pint of good Ale-barm[2];
And when it hath wrought,
Till you perceive the barm to fall,
Then Tun it,
And let it work in the barrel, till the barm
Leaveth rising,
Filling it up every day with some of the same Liquor.
When you stop it up, put in a bag
With one nutmeg sliced,
A little Whole Cloves and Mace,
A stick of Cinnamon broken in pieces,
And a grain of good Musk.

You may make this a little before Michaelmas
And it will be fit to drink
At Lent.

This is Sir Edward Bainton's Receipt,
Which my Lord of Portland (who gave it to me)
Saith,
Was the best he ever drunk.

[1] Carraway
[2] Yeast

112

And from Sir Kenelm's cookery receipts proper, a long-vanished English whey cheese freshly made and eaten with sugar. It must have been much like Italian ricotta, produced in a similar fashion from whey left from a hard-cheese curd:

THE CREAM-COURDS

Strain your whey, and set it on to fire:

Make a clear and gentle fire under the kettle:

As they rise, put in whey, so continuing, till they are ready to skim.

Then take your skimmer, and put them on the bottom of a hair sieve:

So let them drain till they are cold.

Then take them off, and put them into a bason,

And beat them

With three or four spoonfuls of Cream and Sugar.

ELIZABETH DAVID

A July Dinner

A betwixt and between month gastronomically and, too often, a drop in the temperature so that those frost-pearled aspics and palate-chilling salads can remain within the glossy pages of the coffee table cook books, while guests and hosts seek something comfortingly warm. A soup that is equally good hot or chilled can be quickly adapted to the needs of the diners – and taken on a picnic, too.

CUCUMBER SOUP

For four people, coarsely chop half a medium-sized, unpeeled cucumber, half a medium-sized onion and cut up a medium-sized peeled potato. Put them in $\frac{1}{2}$ pint of chicken stock or bouillon, bring to the boil and simmer until tender, or pressure cook for three minutes. Put the vegetables through a food mill or a liquidizer, add salt, pepper, a few finely chopped sprigs of parsley,

½ pint milk, a little grated nutmeg and, if possible, ¼ pint double cream and a squeeze of lemon juice. Bring to the boil if to be served hot, otherwise heat the ingredients gently together before putting them to cool and then chill them thoroughly.

CHICKEN WITH SCAMPI

This recipe was a speciality of the Hotel du Rozier et de la Muse in the Gorges du Tarn, where crayfish out of the river were included. If they cannot be obtained, scampi can be substituted without debasing a fine recipe, as the succulence of the sauce compensates for any slight lack of flavour.

For four people, allow a 2½–3 lb. chicken, and have two small birds for more, not a larger – and less flavourful – fowl. Rub the bird with salt and lemon, put it with 2 oz. of butter in a heavy flameproof casserole with a lid and cook gently for about thirty-five to forty minutes. While this proceeds, sweat a clove of garlic, a sliced onion, three or four tomatoes, a pinch of fennel (or grain of corriander, or a pinch of grated nutmeg), a bouquet garni and salt and pepper in 1½ oz. butter. (For more than four persons, increase quantities by half.) When the vegetables are soft, add ½ pint chicken stock, simmer for five more minutes, then sieve them. Meanwhile, poach the scampi (allowing six per person) for three minutes in boiling water, drain them, put them in a shallow pan, pour a small glass of brandy over them and set light to it. When the flames have died, add the vegetable purée and ¼–½ pint double cream, according to the quantities. Stir well and check as to whether more salt and pepper are required. By now the chicken should be ready to put on the top of the stove. Remove the lid of the casserole, pour a small glass of brandy on the bird and set light to it, spooning the juices over it until the flames die down. Pour the scampi and sauce over the bird, put the lid on the casserole and continue cooking on the top of the stove for ten to fifteen minutes. Serve with the lightest accompaniment – plain boiled potatoes or rice – but allow enough for adequate mopping up of the sauce. Use of anything except the best butter and cream won't justify the effort and expense of making this dish! A nice challenge to the wine lover is to choose the ideal accompaniment.

PRICKLY PEACHES

Cream in the two first courses – even though the lemon and cucumber sharpen it in the soup – means that fresh fruit or a fruity sweet is a 'must'. If the delicately flavoured white fleshed peaches are not available, the yellow fleshed type, being cheaper, justify cooking, or canned peach halves may be used. Peel, halve and pip the peaches, allowing a whole fruit or two halves per person. Stick each one with slivers of toasted almonds, sprinkle with more almonds, a little grated orange peel and, if required, a little caster sugar, pour a tablespoonful of dessert sherry or similar dessert wine over each half and bake in a moderate oven for ten to fifteen minutes. Serve hot or cold.

PAMELA VANDYKE PRICE

A Summer Supper

A summer supper should make the best use of fresh fruit and vegetables, with the colour, texture and temperature of the separate courses varied and complementary, and designed for what we hope will be real July weather. This simple menu for six starts and ends with cold dishes, both of which can be prepared well in advance. It is said that so many cooks are afraid to serve hot soufflé except as a first course: it is extremely difficult to make a failure of this one, and I have safely kept it, without falling, in a warm oven after it was cooked while slow eaters and good talkers finished the first course.

SALAD OF HARICOT VERTS

I first had this dish in Rome made of perfect tiny whole beans. These are often available in Berwick Street Market, Soho, though the salad is equally successful prepared with the larger variety broken in half. It is very attractive served in shallow glass bowls or white gratin dishes, and can be accompanied by hot French bread.

2 lb. haricots verts, two tins anchovy fillets 2 oz. size, a small piece of garlic, 5 tablespoonfuls good fruity olive oil, black pepper, a teaspoonful of lemon juice.

Top and tail the beans and cook them in boiling, salted water until tender. Make the dressing by rubbing a bowl with garlic and working one tin of drained anchovies into the olive oil. Season well with freshly ground black pepper and lemon juice. While the beans are still warm coat them carefully with this dressing. The second tin of drained fillets is used to garnish the salad which should be well chilled.

SMOKED FISH SOUFFLÉ

1½ lb. smoked haddock, 2 oz. butter, 2 oz. plain flour, a good ¼ pint milk, ¼ pint fish stock, white pepper and a little salt, five large eggs and one extra white, 1 tablespoonful grated cheese.

Buy sufficient smoked haddock of the true pale variety to give about 1 lb. when cooked, boned and skinned. Make a Béchamel sauce with the butter, flour, milk and cooking liquor, this last reduced and strained. When the sauce is cool beat in the egg yolks and stir in the flaked fish. Season, taste, and add the cheese. A combination of Parmesan and Gruyère is excellent, but do not despair if all you have in the larder is Cheddar. Butter an 8 inch diameter deep-sided fireproof dish – it is unnecessary to have a soufflé dish to produce a perfect soufflé. Heat oven and baking sheet. Now you can relax and have a drink. Just before serving the Haricots Verts beat the six egg whites and fold them lightly into the fish panada. Turn into the prepared dish, place on baking sheet and cook at approximately gas No. 6, 400°F for twenty-five minutes. Open the oven door and check progress, adjusting the heat up or down as necessary. It is difficult to give a precise temperature or length of time for soufflés as ovens vary so widely, but this dish is perfectly cooked in my Parkinson Cowan after thirty-five minutes at No. 6.

Very small unpeeled English new potatoes make a pleasant accompaniment to this dish and courgettes and skinned tomatoes cooked in butter need the minimum of time and attention.

JEAN GARRETT

More July Food

'A man's dinner in the house of an epicure. The principal dish was cold lamb. At an ordinary "mixed" dinner no host or hostess would dare to offer cold lamb. But this cold lamb was amazing and amazingly sweet. Its reception amply justified the host's courage. Conversation general. Old friends argued abusively in perfect contentment and security. Consumption of alcohol very moderate indeed. We broke up early. If all dinner-parties were as satisfactory –!'

ARNOLD BENNETT *Journal 1929*

With his uncommon gift for describing good food so that his readers are convinced that it was good, Arnold Bennett easily persuaded me that a joint of lamb could make a beautiful cold dish to offer guests. What does seem odd to me is Bennett's assumption that when faced with the unexpected, presented as the precisely right and proper thing, women should be any less receptive than men.

One does, I think, have to make the proviso that a joint of lamb to be eaten cold be of prime quality, and roasted so that it is still pink enough in the centre to retain all its juices; and cooked only in the morning for dinner, or on the evening of the previous day if it is for a lunch party. The joint must be left to cool naturally. If you want it in perfect condition do not consign it to the refrigerator there to spend a night and a day in getting ice into its bones and iron into its flesh. Even when a cooked cold joint is transfered from the refrigerator to a warm room in plenty of time for it to get back to normal temperature, it never quite regains the pristine quality of food freshly cooked, freshly cooled, and eaten before it has completely firmed-up. With cold meat, texture counts every bit as much as flavour.

COLD SADDLE OF LAMB

For my money the best cut of lamb for cold eating is a saddle on the bone, although there is much to be said for a boned and rolled shoulder, a joint which is often the best value for money, and cuts better cold than hot. Whatever the joint chosen, cook it at moderate heat only. Food cooked to be eaten cold should not be subjected to violent temperatures. The average weight of a saddle of lamb is about 6 lb. and should serve at least eight people.

Preheat the oven to gas No. 5, 380°F. Wrap the joint (if the kidneys are included with it keep them for another dish – cold, they would be wasted) in oiled paper or foil, and stand it on a grid placed over a baking tin. Cook it in the centre of the oven for one and a quarter hours. Unwrap it, turn the oven down to No. 3, 330°F, and cook it another half hour. During the final cooking baste the joint with its own juices. Leave the meat, still standing on its rack, to cool. Serve it on a long dish with very fresh watercress arranged at each end.

For an accompaniment to cold lamb there are few dishes to beat a salad of tender, fresh string beans cooked for approximately seven minutes in boiling salted water, drained, and while still warm seasoned and dressed with a mildly fruity olive oil and a little lemon juice. Allow ¼ lb. beans per head. And, ideally, they should be cooked not more than an hour before they are to be eaten.

To precede the cold lamb I should choose either an English cheese pudding, which is much like a soufflé but far less inclined to turn ugly if kept waiting a few minutes, or, for those who know how to make it, and do not flinch before the work involved, an aromatic fish broth, strong, hot, and not too thick.

To finish, I should offer a soft cheese and then a sweet dish – peeled freshly sliced peaches in wine (red or white, dry or sweet, as you please), a vanilla-scented apricot or greengage tart made with a crumbly short pastry or, if the moment were right, which it just sometimes is at some point towards the middle of July, a fruit salad made from raspberries, redcurrants and ripe red gooseberries, a mixture from which arises all the scent of a childhood-remembered English summer fruit garden.

SUMMER FRUIT SALAD

Put 1 lb. of topped and tailed red gooseberries, ¼ lb. of redcurrants and about 6 oz. of white sugar into an enamel-lined or fireproof porcelain saucepan. No water. Simmer the fruit and sugar together for five to seven minutes. Add ½ lb. of raspberries and cook them for two minutes, not a second more. Serve hot, with a jug of cream, cold, thick, but very fresh.

FRESH FIGS WITH ORANGE JUICE

Allow two firm, very slightly under-ripe purple or green figs per person. Cut the stalks from the figs but do not peel them. Quarter them, put them in a bowl, and over them pour the juice, freshly squeezed, of one large or two small oranges for eight figs. No sugar is necessary, but the fruit should be prepared an hour or so before it is to be eaten.

Presented in a perfectly plain white china salad bowl, or in individual clear glass wine goblets, this fig salad is one of the most beautiful as well as one of the most exquisite of all fresh fruit dishes.

ELIZABETH DAVID

Growth of a Food Lover

The discovery of a new dish does more for the happiness of man than the discovery of a star.
BRILLAT-SAVARIN, *Physiologie du Goût*

We all begin life as food eaters but whether we become food lovers is another matter because, in my opinion there is a vast difference between the two.

Circumstances were in my favour when, in 1920, my step-father retired from the Army to his farm in Devonshire. I was fourteen at that time, with the voracious appetite of a schoolboy. Looking back on those years, I now realise how lucky I was. The farm was about 250 acres, bounded on the south by the River Exe and on the north by the Great Western Railway – so there was fishing in the river and train-watching from the local signal box. The land was mixed arable and grazing with Red Devon cattle, Gloucester Old Spot pigs, Rhode Island Red poultry, ducks, geese, and apple orchards with our own cider press. There was also a large, cool dairy with its pans of clotted cream and home-made butter. My mouth waters at the thought of all that fresh food, not forgetting the fruit and vegetables.

May and Rose Cuffe were sisters. May was a superb cook under the enthusiastic guidance of my mother. Rose was the perfect needlewoman and housemaid. Both were my eternal friends, and 50 years since those halcyon days Rose is happily alive and well in the eighty-fourth year of her life, the same gentle friend of my youth.

So, after five years of Devonshire cooking and my sister's French cuisine in Bordeaux, I was ripe for a change, and I endured, without a pang for the past, the sort of food to be found in any Officer's Mess from Lucknow to Colchester. However, in 1941 came the jolt whereby I found myself, via Egypt and Greece, in Germany, on a diet of old potatoes and a modicum of horseflesh, and where one cigarette was the currency of hunger. My companions in prison numbered experts and enthusiasts in every walk of life – a Scotsman taught me to knit, a vast Australian goaded me into becoming a cook. Thus my only claim to fame during the war was the invention of a dish ironically named 'Bull Shit Pie' evolved from the rare but highly prized contents of a Canadian Red Cross parcel. I won't give you the recipe – but on its rare appearances it was awarded the Cordon Bleu of its time and place!

Back in England in 1945, the spark had been kindled, and I joined an all male cookery class which met at 6 pm somewhere near Victoria Station. We behaved disgracefully, and almost reduced our attractive female tutor to tears by our outrageous teasing and leg-pulling. Nevertheless, she achieved something. I took up cooking!

In 1951 there appeared in the shops a book entitled *French Country Cooking* and I bought my first cookery book. A few years later, thanks to a mutual friend, it was my good fortune to meet the author. Then, one fine Sunday, my mother and I were privileged to eat a meal in the author's kitchen – a meal which turned us both from food eaters into food lovers. Our hostess was Elizabeth David. I won't attempt to describe the food; but what lingers in my memory to this day was its simplicity – and the delightful informality of the setting and of the occasion.

From that day stemmed a genuine interest in cookery, which, though it may have waxed and waned, has never really deserted me. I would add that my mother continued to cook and do her own shopping right up to the age of eighty-nine.

Without the help, council and friendship of Elizabeth David I would never have attempted the task of editing and compiling the *Wine and Food Leaflets* which go to make up this book.

August

In a field among the woods the flax sheaves stood in shocks
like wheat, the fine-hung bells on their wiry hair stalks
rustling and quaking in the breeze like wag wantons. A mare
and foal stood in the shade among the flax sheaves.

FRANCIS KILVERT 1871

Without comment

It is an economic axiom as old as the hills that goods and services can be paid for only with goods and services.
ALBERT JAY NOCK, 1873–1945

'The Wine in the bottle is almost the least of what the good Wine Merchant sells you. Invisibly there are his expertise and long years of experience, his faith in the wines he has chosen and bought, and his assessment of what you want in a wine. He will discuss with you which ones to choose for which occasion, how he expects his wines to develop and guide you to lay by advantageously your wines for the future.

'He will bring your wine to your door, he will store your young wine and deliver it when it is ready. He will provide glasses for your party, decant an old bottle for your dinner, and even give you credit!

'We say all this because, after the recent hulabaloo over price cutting, we feel it should be underlined, what all true wine lovers know, that you get the Wine Merchant you deserve. And if his customers don't support him now in any price cutting war, they won't deserve him and further more they won't get him, for he will go out of existence. He cannot compete today, with his heavy overheads and narrow margins of profit, with supermarkets who can afford to lose money (for a short time) on some commodity like wine while making their profit on other goods. Now is the time to support him!' Extract from editorial of *Wine Magazine*[1].

The long arm of coincidence

A man, sir, should keep his friendship in constant repair.
BOSWELL, *Life of Johnson.* 1755
Quis Separabit?
Motto of the P & O Steam Navigation Company

In February I told my friend Rudi Heyman, shipper of German and French wine, of my plan to spend a holiday in Gibraltar and

[1] Wine and Spirit Publications Ltd, South Bank House, Black Prince Road, London, SE1.

visit one of my oldest friends who lives there. Of course I would travel P & O, I added, and told him why.

Peninsular and Oriental Steam Navigation – how the proud title rolls off the tongue, and what an important part their splendid ships have played in my life and friendships, and in the lives of countless other men and women. In 1925 I sailed from Southampton in the *Ranchi*, for Bombay to join my Regiment in Lucknow, and to make there two of my oldest and closest friendships. In 1928 I went home on leave travelling POSH – Port out, Starboard home – in the *Rawalpindi*, of glorious memory to all who remember her epic single-handed battle with the *Scharnhorst* and *Gneisenau* in 1939. Little did I know that many years later my mother would become a friend of Mrs Kennedy, widow of Captain E. C. Kennedy, RN who commanded, and died with, HMS *Rawalpindi* and her crew. In 1940 the *Orcades* carried me and friends via the Cape of Good Hope to Suez and the Middle East, and thence, by other devious and curious means of transport, to new and lasting friendships. The P & O gave of the total tonnage of their ships, and of the gallant men who served in them, more than one half in the last war.

It is a far cry from *William Fawcett*, the 206-ton paddle steamer, with which Willcox and Anderson founded the Peninsular Steam Navigation Co. in 1837 to the *Canberra*, the 45,700 ton turbo-electric steamship, the beautiful and luxurious flagship of the Peninsular and Orient Lines of 1967. But it was those early friendships and loyalties to the Royal Houses of Portugal and Spain that brought the original Company the valuable trading facilities on which the vast present-day fleet is founded, with the right to use their colours which form the quarterings of their House Flag, blue and white for Portugal, red and yellow for Spain.

On 30th May I walked up the gangway of the *Canberra*, forty-two years after my first voyage in the *Ranchi*, *en route* for Gibraltar. As the call went out, 'All Visitors Ashore', I stood on the foredeck just below the bridge of the *Canberra*, above which flew the flags of her house, Blue Peter and the Royal Mail. Memories of old and new friendships came flooding back in her proud motto, 'Who shall dare to separate us', and my heart was filled with regret for neglecting so many of them. This bond between two human being is priceless; it should be like a rare and well-worn piece of silver, to be frequently handled and looked at lovingly, kept bright and polished against the hazards of life and never kept in a drawer where its presence is taken for granted.

Behind me Rudi Heyman was dead, mourned by all who had cherished the warmth and generosity of his humanity. Ahead of me at Gibraltar was one of those two friends of 1925 whom I knew I was to see for the last time. The *Canberra* slid silently from the quay and once more the P & O was carrying me to a new friend of whose existence I knew nothing but to whose reality I now say thank you.

Wine Friendships

At my age it is natural to stick to my old and faithful friends in the wine trade. But I did take an instant liking to Dr Wilhelm Reitz of Mainz and his wines, which, I am confident, will gain the friendship of our customers, once they have tasted them.

In the province of Baden, viticulture stretches over an area of sixty kilometres from north to south, and three quarters of the total area is in the south, of which the Kaiserstuhl district takes the biggest share. Kaiserstuhl is a mountainous volcanic islet on the Rhine plain (about twelve miles north-west of Freiburg) where Baden's best wines are made. Their success is owed to the Rulander grape (Pinot Gris), which has found here a suitable soil, and which produces big, spicy, velvety wines. Fine wines are also made from the Ortenau, the name of a region stretching, in a number of separate small districts, from Ortenberg, south of Offenberg, via Durbach into the hill and river district of Achern.

KATZENSTRIEGEL, N.V.	13/6
KAISERSTUHL–TUNIBERG RIESLING X SILVANER,	
OPFINGER SONNENBERG, NATUR 1964	15/6
KAISERSTUHL RULANDER, LEISELHEIMER	
GESTUHL 1964	16/–
ORTENAUER RIESLING, SINZHEIMER	
FRUHMESSLER, NATUR 1964	16/6

August 1967

Gastronomic Pornography

A Song by ADRIAN MITCHELL[1]

Anchovies in aspic
With marinated aubergines.
Beetroot bellies in brandy
With a bucket of Heinz Baked Beans.
Alligator purée and I don't care
If you stuff it with reindeer rind,
But gastronomic pornography
Is booting me out of my mind.

Caviar and cake mix
Makes coriander chocolate cheese.
Chutneyed carrots and coffee –
Won't you slice me a doorstep please?
Pass me down a mousse with its antlers on –
You can cook it in fairy snow,
For gastronomic pornography
Is dragging me down so low.

Gammon stuffed with garlic,
Geraniums and gooseberry fool.
Grouse, gazpacho and ginger,
Burn your kitchen and leave to cool.
I want Mrs Beeton to be my man,
And Elizabeth David too,
For gastronomic pornography
Makes my stomach feel like a zoo.

With the plethora of fancy recipes and frozen foods which confront us wherever we open a newspaper, let alone the glossies or a colour supplement, I sometimes yearn with Adrian Mitchell for a return to that simplicity in cooking which usually conceals considerable expertise, or for what Raymond Postgate called 'The Society for the Prevention of Cruelty to food'!

[1]Reproduced by courtesy of *The Listener*. Adrian Mitchell's latest book of poems *Out Loud* is published in a paperback by Cape Goliard, 12s. od.

The Food for August

LETTUCE

Cooked lettuce is one of the most delicate and refreshing of all summer vegetable dishes. It is also one of the cheapest. Even allowing for the shrinkage in cooking – about equal to that of spinach – a whole large lettuce of the Webbs Wonder variety should be enough for three people. The outer leaves of say two or three lettuces of which the hearts have gone into a salad will produce about the equivalent amount and will cost nothing more than the butter and the fuel required for the cooking. Classic and professional French recipes for braised lettuce do, it is true, call for whole lettuces to be blanched, then stewed very slowly and for a long time (cos lettuce is the best for these recipes) with the addition of clear stock or meat glaze, all of which complicates matters unnecessarily, and makes an expensive although interesting dish. The simple, quick and economical way to cook lettuce is as follows:

Having washed and drained the lettuce, divide the leaves into bundles of five or six. Roll them, and with a sharp stainless-steel knife slice them into fine strips, as though you were slicing a sausage. Simply cook this shredded lettuce in a little butter (1 oz. is ample for a whole lettuce) in an uncovered sauté pan or flameproof casserole for about five minutes. Season with a pinch of sugar as well as salt and a scrap of grated nutmeg.

Lettuce cooked in this way is delicious with veal, with fish, with eggs, and as a basis for summer soups.

EGGS EN COCOTTE WITH LETTUCE AND CREAM

For each person allow 2 tablespoonfuls of lettuce cooked as described above, 2 tablespoonfuls of cream mixed with a heaped teaspoonful of grated Parmesan, one or two eggs, a walnut of butter.

Put the cooked lettuce, with a knob of fresh butter, into individual egg ramekins or cocottes. Heat gently. Break the eggs into cups. Transfer them to the cocottes. Pour the cream and cheese mixture round them. Put small plates or lids over the egg dishes. If these are china or glazed earthenware put them into a shallow pan of water on top of the stove or on a baking sheet in a moderate oven. If they are enamelled cast-iron or enamelled steel use them over direct but very moderate heat.

The eggs will take four to eight minutes to cook, depending upon the type and size of dish used and the degree of heat.

Remove the dishes from the oven, hot-water pan or hot-plate before the whites are completely set. By the time they are brought to the table they will be just right. The lettuce, cream and egg combined is a very fresh tasting and original one.

PLUMS

Among the home-grown plums which are the treats of late summer, the true greengage is incomparably the finest dessert fruit, while purple Pershores are one of the best varieties for jams and pies. Then there are Monarchs, Czars, Presidents (whatever happened to the Moguls and the Impératrices?), imported Switzers, the Yugoslav version of the quetsch, and home-grown Victorias, all good for preserves and for slow baking, a method which produces cooked plums at their best, richly flavoured and with a small amount of fine dark juice.

PLUMS BAKED IN WINE

1 lb. Victoria, Czar or other good cooking plums, 3 tablespoon-fuls of sugar, 2 tablespoonfuls each of port wine and water.

The plums should be, preferably, slightly under-ripe. Wipe them with a soft cloth. With a fruit knife make a slit in each plum, following the natural division of the fruit.

In a baking dish (I use a deepish fireproof china bowl – one of the thick, white French Pilivuyt salad bowls which are also useful for oven-cooking – but almost any baking dish will do provided it is not too large for the quantity of fruit. This should, if possible, be piled up rather than spread out in one layer), put the fruit, strewn with sugar, which can be brown, white or vanilla-flavoured; alternatively, a vanilla pod can be cooked with the fruit. Add the wine and water. Bake near the top of a slow oven, gas No. 2, 210°F, for thirty-five to forty minutes. The timing depends upon the variety and relative ripeness of the plums. They should be tender but still retain their shape. They are delicious hot or cold.

The recipes above are from the newly revised and recently published Penguin edition (1965) of Elizabeth David's *Summer Cooking*, first published by Museum Press 1955.

MOUSSE DE JAMBON

The great gastronomical treat of August is roast grouse. Whether it is better hot or cold, whether one should accompany it by one's best Claret or one's best burgundy is a perennial problem, as hard to decide as whether one prefers strawberries to raspberries. But alas! one cannot, for various reasons, eat grouse at every meal in the month. So, on the assumption that some days may be hot, here are two cold dishes, a meat dish and a pudding, which are suitable for August.

1 lb. raw gammon, ⅓ pint double cream, 1 teaspoonful dry mustard, black pepper, nutmeg, a dash of brandy, three egg whites.

Remove all the fat from the gammon, chop the lean, pound it and put it through a sieve. Stir in the cream, brandy and season-ings. Whip the egg whites – not too stiff – and fold them in. Put the mixture into a buttered soufflé (or similarly shaped) dish, smooth the top and cover with a buttered greaseproof paper and then with a plate or lid. Cook in a bain-marie in a moderate oven for about forty minutes. Allow to cool and place in the refrigerator for two to three hours.

An alternative recipe, and perhaps easier, is as follows:

1 lb. cooked ham, ⅓ pint Béchamel sauce, pepper and paprika, ¼ pint melted aspic jelly, ⅔ pint cream.

Remove the fat from the ham, mince the lean and pound it with the Béchamel. Put it through a sieve and work it in a bowl on ice for a few minutes, mixing in the aspic slowly. Lightly whip the cream and fold it into the mixture. Turn it into a soufflé-dish and put it in the refrigerator for several hours.

And with the Ham Mousse a green salad.

My old friend, Mrs Carter, could make a pudding as well as translate Epictetus.

SAMUEL JOHNSON, 1709–84

SUMMER PUDDING

Butter some bread and cut it as thin as for bread-and-butter. Cut off the crusts and line a pudding-basin with the bread-and-butter with the butter side to the basin. Stew blackcurrants with white sugar and a very little water. Half fill the basin with the currants and a little juice. Cover them with a layer of unbuttered bread. Fill up with more currants and juice and cover with another layer of thin unbuttered bread. Put a plate on top and put a weight on the plate so that the juice is pressed into the bread. Leave for twenty-fours so that the bread gets saturated. Turn and and cover with whipped cream.

You may prefer summer pudding made of raspberries and red-currants. If you do, stew them together and proceed in the same way. Some prefer raspberries alone. I do not think it is necessary to cook them: put the raspberries in a bowl, sprinkle caster sugar on them and let them stand for a few hours (the sugar will bring out the juice).

ROBIN MCDOUALL

Picnics . . .

I am addicted to picnics. I love the planning of what food to buy and prepare, and how it is to be packed – even though disaster is predicted in the shape of the weather forecast.

My basket, of venerable age, came from the Lord Roberts workshop for Disabled Ex-service men in the Brompton Road, specialists in picnic gear. My containers are two large-size thermos jars, with ample room for ice, butter, pâté, or anything that melts, and are equally good for hot soup or stew. Thermos flasks or better still the jugs look after the liquids, hot or cold. Then there are the plastic boxes for the little snacks of salami sausage, radishes, olives, cheese and fruits; and lastly good and cheap glasses from Woolworths for the rough red wine or rosé, reserving the plastic mugs for the tea or coffee. Here are two picnic dishes easily prepared the day before.

SMOKED COD'S ROE PASTE

Turn the contents of a 6 oz. jar of smoked cod's roe into a bowl and pour over it 4 tablespoonfuls of water. Leave for an hour or two. The water will soften the roe, make it easier to work, and desalt it a little. Pound a clove of garlic in a mortar. Drain off excess liquid from the cod's roe, which you now beat with the garlic in your mixer, adding about 4 tablespoonfuls of olive oil, the juice of half a lemon and 2–3 tablespoonfuls of water.

The paste should be the consistency of thick cream. If you prefer it thicker or find it too salt add the crumb of white bread first softened in water and squeezed dry. A tablespoonful of mashed potato serves the same purpose. Keep in the fridge overnight and then transfer into a round plastic container which will fit, on top of some ice, into your thermos jar. Spread on buttered wholemeal bread.

Summer Cooking

TERRINE OF HAM, PORK AND VEAL

1 lb. each of ham (cooked), pork and veal (raw); white wine, brandy, garlic, bayleaves, ¼ lb. bacon, mace, pepper, salt, juniper berries, thyme, marjoram. Mince the pork and veal,

cut the ham into small squares. Mix all together, add a clove of garlic chopped with five or six juniper berries, a little fresh thyme, marjoram, coarsely ground black pepper, about half a teaspoonful of mace, and a very little salt, as the ham will probably be salty. Put the whole mixture into a bowl and pour over a small glass of white wine and 2 tablespoonfuls of brandy. Leave for an hour or two. Cover the bottom of a fairly shallow terrine with little strips of bacon about 2 inches long. Put in the meat mixture, cover with more little strips of bacon and one or two bayleafs in the centre. Put the terrine in a baking dish filled with water and bake in a slow oven for $2\frac{1}{2}$–3 hours. Leave to cool. Eat with crusty bread, lettuce and radishes.

Summer Cooking

. . . and outdoor meals

August is summer at its peak, and evokes long, cool Americanos, one's easiest clothes, outdoor meals and hazy, lazy days. In practice few of these dreams materialize, though without doubt August can produce summer food at its best, fresh and delicate. Not for the home cook the horrors of hotel salads of wilted lettuce awash with malt vinegar and commercial salad cream! In summer months no one need eat tinned or frozen vegetables when they are available fresh even in towns. Overworked and overgarnished cold dishes miss the whole point of summer cooking. Cold food is best served on the day of preparation and not left to lose flavour in the refrigerator. Absolutely dry fresh herbs can be kept for a suprisingly long time in airtight containers, and will add all the flavour of a garden to your cooking.

Salade Niçoise dressed at the table makes a perfect main course for a light summer luncheon to follow, perhaps, a fresh herb omelette. My favourite Niçoise contains lettuce hearts, lightly cooked and cooled French beans, anchovy fillets, mild onion rings and stoned black olives. Hors d'oeuvres should be kept as simple as possible, not more than three or four different ingredients attractively arranged, the oil dressing very light and the mayonnaise thinned with boiling water or single cream. Enough mayonnaise can be made for several days and stored in a cool place. If it separates it can be rescued miraculously by breaking another egg yolk into a clean bowl and slowly adding the curdled emulsion.

Paper-thin slices of rare roast beef are good rolled round very mild home-made creamy horseradish, and served with chilled tomato salad in an oil and lemon dressing with lots of chopped mint. Fresh little English courgettes (still young enough to be hairy) are lovely on their own, sliced thick and cooked unpeeled in butter. Fresh strawberries piled in a glass bowl and covered with orange slices and orange juice are more refreshing than strawberries and cream, and a purée of raspberries and redcurrants has all the scent of summer. For more formal meals fresh poached peaches, skinned and glazed and set on a melting base of pâté sucrée are worth the trouble.

SUMMER SAUCE

Here is a perfect green summer sauce to serve with cold, drained globe artichokes from which the inedible chokes have been removed and a spoonful of sauce poured into each heart – the remainder of the sauce being served in a jug and used for dipping the leaf bases. Half clove crushed garlic, a very little finely chopped onion, salt, freshly ground black pepper and a pinch of sugar, 2 teaspoonfuls rinsed, chopped capers, 8 tablespoonfuls fruity olive oil, 1 tablespoonful wine or tarragon vinegar and a large handful of very finely chopped parsley. Mix all together and chill.

FISH MAYONNAISE

Fish mayonnaise makes a lovely summer party dish. For six you need enough home-made mayonnaise to coat 1 lb. fresh white poached fillet, ½ lb. flaked salmon, the flesh of one crab, a dozen large unshelled prawns for decoration and a diced, well-drained cucumber. Mix all together carefully, arrange on a long white dish and garnish with snipped chives.

Finish the meal with a Petit Suisse for each person placed in a glass and covered with chilled, fresh raspberry purée.

JEAN GARRETT

September

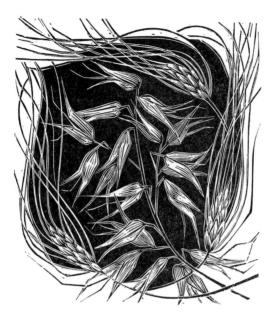

As I walked along the field path I stopped to listen
to the rustle and solemn night whisper of the
wheat, so different to its voice by day. The corn
seemed to be praising God and whispering its
evening prayer. Across the great level meads near
Chippenham came the martial music of a drum
and fife band, and laughing voices of unseen girls
were wafted from farms and hayfields out of the
wide dusk.

FRANCIS KILVERT 1873

In praise of Britain . . .

Heading for the West Country for my summer holiday I admit to a touch of that communal melancholia from which Britain appears to be suffering; and what with our detractors at home and abroad it was all the more refreshing to read Brian Hollowood's editorial in *Punch*. 'Let us now praise things at home' (29th June), and Lord Watkinson's 'Businessmen who deliver the Goods' in *Readers Digest*. On my way to St Mawes I made my usual diversion to stand on The Hoe at Plymouth, and what better place on which to salute Miss Sheila Scott's solo flight round the world. As Sir Alan Cobham said, 'This competes with Drake.' Our thanks are also due to David Koetser for his generous praise of Britain and gift of Titian's *Allegory of Prudence* to the National Gallery as 'a useful gesture in a time of economic stress and strain' – some gesture!

In the Plymouth area I give high praise to Leslie Hoare of the Exeter Inn (fifteenth century) at Modbury for his beautiful dining room and superb dinner. At Pillaton, the Cawthorns of the Weary Friar, formerly a twelfth-century rest-house for travelling friars, offer delicious light meals in unique and comfortable surroundings. If Costa Brava cooks can do better I will eat my Mexican straw hat!

. . . and of freedom

'Take these men for your example. Like them, remember that prosperity can only be for the free; that freedom is the sure possession of those alone who have the courage to defend it.'
From the funeral oration of Pericles, 429 B C

On Sunday, 19th May, I travelled up to London by train with my wife and her Australian friend Joan Stanford. With us in the carriage were her brother Ross Stanford and his wife, and five Australian men. These six men were old comrades from No. 617 Squadon, RAF, and we were on our way to St Clement Danes to a Service of Thanksgiving to commemorate that day, 16th May 1943, when nineteen Lancasters took off for the attack on the Mohne and Eder dams in the Ruhr. Flying at sixty feet above the water, and using the bouncing mine which had been devised by Sir Barnes Wallis, the squadron broke both dams. Eight aircraft and fifty-three men were lost. I was proud to be the guest of these men who had flown all the way from Australia for the 25th anniversary of 'The Dam Busters'.

The world is a strange place! That Sunday also saw the first outbreak of violence in Paris which was to lead to near-anarchy in France, shortly to be followed by the tragic assassination of Senator Robert Kennedy and the rule of the gun in the United States of America. But even if some of us were tempted to scoff at de Gaulle's policy of greatness, as if greatness were something to be ashamed of, the British are a tolerant and magnanimous people, and I fervently hope that our neighbour and friend, even though she may be a temperamental and obstinate one, will quickly regain her democratic freedom and greatness.

That night, the words from the funeral oration of Pericles rang in my ears, to remind me of the example of 'The Dam Busters' and their defence of our freedom, and that Britain, despite taxation and those who prefer exile in the villas of Portugal or Spain, is still the finest country in the world to live in today.

Fortunately for us, rioting in this country is more likely to be carried out at Wembley stadium by mini-skirted screamers with nothing more dangerous than flowers in their hands, to greet the return of Mick Jagger and the Rolling Stones – or, as we still have freedom of choice, at The Royal Albert Hall to welcome Miss Leontyne Price from Laurel, Mississippi. Personally, I shall be at the Albert Hall, with a bouquet of flowers, shouting for Miss Price, the coloured prima donna. 'They come no greater; few anywhere near so great,' says the critic of the *Washington Post and Times Herald*, and I whole-heartedly agree with him!

The prima donnas of dry French white wines come from Burgundy – and because they are rarities they must, like Miss Price, be great. They are difficult to find because, like great singers, they do not grow on trees! For your criticism and choice here are a trio of great single vineyard wines from Puligny Montrachet, bottled at the Domaine.

PULIGNY-MONTRACHET, Les Folatières, 1966   37/-
PULIGNY-MONTRACHET, Clos de la Garenne, 1966   37/6
PULIGNY-MONTRACHET, Clos du Chaniot, 1966   38/6

THE PRIMA DONNA TRIO

When, after completing her musical education, Miss Price returned to her tiny home town to sing for them, she said, 'For an hour and a half we weren't white and black, we were just human beings together.' In her honour I offer three special dry white wines from France.

RIESLING RÉSERVE EXCEPTIONELLE, Alsace, 1966   31/9
CH. DE TRACY, Pouilly Blanc Fumé, 1966   32/-
MEURSAULT LES CASSE TÊTES, 1966   36/-

September 1968

A September Luncheon

I usually find it impossible to visualize the circumstances in which I would buy for, cook and serve a suggested menu from a magazine, so the food for this month is planned for a Sunday luncheon party we are giving in September for eight tanned friends. It can be cooked on Saturday, leaving us free before our guests arrive to go to church or read the papers in bed! All the dishes are cold and contrast well with each other, and the main course is particularly colourful, as befits a dramatically colourful month.

PATÉ

¾ lb. chicken livers, ¼ lb. unsalted butter, one clove garlic, salt and black pepper, good pinch mixed spice and the same of powdered herbs, 1 desertspoonful brandy, 1 teacupful white breadcrumbs, four well-grilled rashers bacon.

Carefully clean the livers cutting out any yellow strains. Sauté them gently in butter for about five minutes with the crushed garlic. Add seasoning, spice and herbs. Pour in the brandy and allow to bubble. Put this mixture through the liquidizer. Beat in the breadcrumbs and stir in the bacon, snipped into tiny pieces. Cover with foil and leave overnight in the refrigerator. Serve slightly chilled with hot rolls or toast.

SUMMER CHICKEN

Two good chickens, half a lemon, two carrots, two onions, one stick celery, boquet garni, seasoning, one large glass white wine.

Poach the chickens very gently until tender with the lemon, vegetables, herbs and wine in sufficient water, to cover. When cold, remove birds and take all the meat off the bones, cutting into good sized pieces. Arrange the meat on a large serving dish and make the sauce.

Two egg yolks, $\frac{1}{2}$ pint double cream, $\frac{1}{2}$ pint strained chicken stock from which the fat has been removed, I tablespoonful lemon juice, grated rind one lemon. Beat egg yolks into cream and stir into heated stock. Cook gently, stirring all the time, until slightly thick but do not allow to boil. Remove from heat and add lemon juice. Pour over chicken and scatter with grated lemon rind. The sauce will thicken as it gets cold. Cover with foil and keep cool. Now make the rice salad.

I lb. patna rice, 2 tablespoonfuls olive oil, 2 teaspoonfuls wine vinegar, salt and black pepper, grated nutmeg, four large tomatoes, one celery heart, one green and one red pimento, $\frac{1}{2}$ lb. cooked shelled peas, $\frac{1}{2}$ lb. small black olives, one cucumber.

Cook rice for about twelve minutes and drain well. Stir in the oil and vinegar immediately and season with salt, pepper and nutmeg. With two forks carefully mix into the rice the unpeeled tomatoes cut into segments, the chopped celery and pimentos, the peas and olives. Pile the rice salad on a large platter and cover with foil. Keep cool for the night. The next day peel the cucumber and run a fork down its length all the way round. Cut into thin slices and lay these overlapping each other round the rice salad.

This is a very spectacular dish and simple to make though it takes time. It was first served me many years ago in Rutland Gate by a Swedish lady and I have used it with great success thereafter. The delightful contrast of nutty, crunchy salad and the bland gentle chicken sauce is particularly attractive.

Follow this with a dessert of the utmost simplicity and gorgeous hue.

BLACKBERRIES AND CREAM

2½ lb. cultivated blackberries, 6 oz. granulated sugar. Stew the blackberries in sugar very, very carefully without any water. They will make a thick little syrup of their own. Pour into a glass dish and add a squeeze of lemon. Serve very cold and hand single cream.

JEAN GARRETT

Skins

By the time you read this, 'The Battle of the Tan' has been fought for some months and thousands of pounds have been spent on getting to your favourite beaches and on lotions and oils. During the battle one can guess at the sufferings of Shadrach, Meshach and Abednego; in addition to frayed nerves, lost tempers, unbearable contact with spouse or other human beings, even wooden frames may have been used to raise the bed clothes from burning flesh!

Skins will have become piebald, dark brown hands and face, lighter brown forearms and legs, reddish upper arms and white buttocks. In women the effect is even more bizarre and the absurdity is heightened by two white mounds like reverse chromium headlamps adorning the upper part of the body. Thank goodness the effect is only temporary!

'The Battle of the Grape Skin' is much more serious; the health, texture, colour and bloom of this skin is essential to the making of good wine. In the month of September the victory of the natural ferments, or yeast cells, which form on the outside of grape skins at the time of their full maturity is vital to your future enjoyment of quality wine and is worth far more to you than the temporary victory of the costly creams, unguents and lotions over suffering Anglo-Saxon Skins!

Let us hope for a bountiful harvest of healthy grape skins and the precious juice they contain!

Oysters

'Never eat an oyster unless there is an R in the month' – is good advice and limits the eating of oysters to the months from September to April inclusive. The legal close-time for oysters in England and Scotland, however, extends only from 15th June to 4th August.

'Who eats oysters on St. James's Day will never want' – St James's Day is the first day of the oyster season (5th August) when oysters are an expensive luxury only eaten by the rich. But in Dicken's day this was not the case. *'It's a wery remarkable circumstance, sir,'* said Sam, *'that poverty and oysters always seem to go together.'*

It is also a very remarkable circumstance that Chablis has taken on a loose generic meaning of 'dry white wine'. It is sad that there are so many who have had the name of the commune frequently on their lips and rarely its wine on their palates.

True Chablis is light and dry and fragrant with a clean pebbly bouquet. The appellation is not confined to Chablis alone, and covers an area including a number of neighbouring communes. The négociants of Chablis prefer to blend their premiers crûs to make a quantity more commercially convenient and it is, there-fore, rare to find premiers crûs unblended.

A September Dinner

Start a September meal with a surprise – tiny, pale kippers from the Isle of Man, served raw with brown bread, butter and lemon; like smoked salmon but so pleasantly different, and so cheap. Follow this with a salad vegetable made into a hot soup.

CREAM OF LETTUCE SOUP

Melt 1 oz. of butter in a heavy pan and add a large, shredded head of lettuce – the cabbage kind is best – and one small finely chopped onion. Cover and cook over a low heat for five minutes. Blend in 2 teaspoonfuls of flour and season with salt, pepper, a pinch of sugar and a little freshly grated nutmeg. Add ¾ pint of chicken stock and simmer for ten to fifteen minutes. Put through a blender or rub through a sieve. Reheat with ½ pint of milk and, when hot, add two egg yolks beaten with 4 tablespoonfuls of cream. Reheat without boiling and sprinkle with finely chopped parsley or, better, with mint. (A squeeze of lemon juice will give a pleasantly sharp taste.) Hand little croûtons of fried bread with this.

VEAL AMANDINE

Buy 1½ lb. of fillet of veal and cut it into small, thin, roundish slices. Heat 1½ oz. of butter gently in a frying pan and cook the veal lightly in it for five minutes till lightly brown on both sides. Add 5 tablespoonfuls of white wine and 2 teaspoonfuls of lemon juice and season to taste. (If possible, add a good teaspoonful of chopped fresh lemon thyme or marjoram.) Cook gently for another five minutes, shaking the pan from time to time. Now pour in the contents of two cartons of soured cream. Heat through, over a low heat. Simmer for a further five minutes and, before serving, sprinkle with 3 oz. of split and toasted blanched almonds. Serve with new potatoes and green beans.

BAKED PEACHES IN ZABAGLIONE SAUCE

Each year the Italian peach season gets longer and this year peaches should be cheaper than ever. Picked before they are ripe, so that they do not deteriorate *en route*, they are often better served cooked and hot.

For each person take a large peach and bake in sugar syrup in a low oven for twenty to thirty minutes; cool a little, skin, halve and stone. Put back in the syrup to keep warm.

While they are cooking, put three egg yolks – for four people – into a bowl with 6 teaspoonfuls of vanilla sugar, 1 teaspoonful of grated lemon rind and 3 tablespoonfuls of Marsala. Beat over simmering water until the mixture froths and rises up in the pan and is thick enough to hold the mark of the whisk. Remove from the heat.

Now put the peaches in individual dishes, pour the zabaglione over them and sprinkle with crushed ratafias or amaretti.

This is also very good cold. Chill the zabaglione and, if you wish to make it go further, fold in, just before serving, two stiffly beaten egg whites.

MARGARET COSTA

144

More September Food

A strongly flavoured, aromatically scented meat and vegetable stew called Pebronata, a dish of Corsican origin, provides an interesting and little known way of cooking the green peppers which are now obtainable in England nearly all the year round, but which are at their best and cheapest in the early autumn.

First, the sauce is prepared in the following manner.

Ingredients are one small and one large onion, one large or two small cloves of garlic, a tablespoonful of chopped parsley, a branch of dried thyme or a half teaspoonful of dried or fresh thyme leaves, 1 lb. of very ripe tomatoes, 4 tablespoonfuls of olive oil, six small green peppers or two or three larger ones, a glass (4–6 oz.) of rough red wine, a heaped teaspoonful of flour, salt, a half-dozen juniper berries.

Chop the small onion together with the parsley and garlic. Heat 2 tablespoonfuls of the olive oil in a shallow pan. Put in the onion and garlic mixture. Add the thyme. After five minutes' gentle cooking put in the tomatoes, unskinned but roughly chopped. Season with salt. Add the crushed juniper berries. Simmer steadily for about fifteen to twenty minutes.

Meanwhile peel and slice the large onion. Put it in another pan with the remaining 2 tablespoonfuls of warmed olive oil.

Let it melt very gently. When the onion is yellow and soft add the green peppers, washed (all seeds and core discarded) and sliced into, roughly, 1 inch lengths. When the peppers are slightly softened, stir in the flour, then add the red wine, heated in a separate saucepan. Stir well, let the wine reduce by two thirds.

Now press the tomato sauce through a fine sieve into a bowl. Pour the resulting purée into the green pepper and wine mixture. Cook gently for another five minutes or so. The peppers should not be too soft.

Now for the stew itself.

Allow about 2 lb. of a cheap cut of beef (top rump, thick flank, or shin). Cut the meat into cubes. Brown them in olive oil. Add seasonings, a sprig or two of dry thyme, a couple of bayleaves and a glass (about 6 oz.) of white wine. (Or, if more convenient, more of the same red wine used for making the sauce.) Cover the pot.

Cook very slowly for $1\frac{1}{2}$–2 hours, or until the meat is tender.

Now add the prepared Pebronata sauce and cook for another twenty to thirty minutes. Serve with plain boiled or mashed potatoes or with ribbon noodles or rice.

While muscat grapes are in season, they can be combined with other – and cheaper – fresh fruit to make beautiful and refreshing fruit salads.

MELON AND MUSCAT GRAPES

Green-fleshed, yellow-skinned honeydew melons are best for this mixture. Cut the melon in quarters, discard seeds and rind. Slice the flesh into cubes. Put these into a bowl, squeeze lemon juice over them, stew them with sugar. Add a handful of peeled and seeded muscat grapes – or, when they are available, the tiny little white currant grapes imported from Greece or Cyprus, which are eaten skin and all, and need only be stripped from the stalks and washed before they are added to the fruit salad.

HONEY AND WALNUT CREAM

A Provençal honey recipe.

Pound or chop finely 3 oz. walnuts, shelled weight. Mix with them 2 tablespoonfuls of thick aromatic honey (Provence honey from Forcalquiet is obtainable from Harrods – at a price. Our own heather or clover honey is just as good for this recipe) and 2 tablespoonfuls of thick cream.

Spread between thin buttered slices of fresh brown bread, this mixture makes exquisite little sandwiches for tea, or to serve instead of wafers or biscuits with a lemon or apricot ice-cream.

This amount makes about a dozen little sandwiches but the mixture keeps a long time in a covered jar, so it can be made in larger quantities.

Mediterranean Food

GRATIN DE RIZ ET DE COURGETTES

This recipe was given to me by the proprietor of a village inn near Aix-en-Provence. I have never encountered the dish anywhere else, nor seen it described in any cookery book.

For two people: ½ lb. of courgettes, 3 oz. butter, 3 tablespoonfuls of uncooked Patna or Italian rice, a tablespoonful of flour, 8 oz. of milk (½ pint minus 2 oz.), 2 teaspoonfuls of grated Parmesan cheese, seasonings.

Pare the courgettes, cut them into cubes, put them into a frying pan with a sprinkling of salt. Cover the pan and cook extremely gently without any liquid whatsoever, for about fifteen minutes. By this time the salt and the heat will have drawn the moisture from the courgettes. Let it evaporate with the pan uncovered before adding 1½ oz. of butter. Now cook, still very gently, for a further fifteen minutes or so, and uncovered, until the courgettes are pale golden – not browned – and quite soft.

Meanwhile, cook the rice in a saucepan of boiling salted water, keeping it on the firm side. Drain it.

Make a Béchamel sauce with 1 oz. of butter, the flour and the warmed milk. Season it, let it cook over a mat, for fifteen minutes. Stir in 1 teaspoonful of the cheese. Add the courgettes. Stir all together, for a few seconds, and then sieve the mixture or purée it in the electric blender.

Have ready a very lightly buttered gratin dish, cover the bottom of it with a thin layer of the purée, mix the rest with the rice put it all into the dish and, lightly, smooth it down. On top sprinkle the remaining teaspoonful of cheese and the rest of the butter in tiny knobs.

Put the dish near the top of a very moderate oven, gas No. 3, 330°F, and leave it for thirty minutes if the whole mixture is to be heated up from cold, or for fifteen to twenty minutes if it has just been prepared and is still hot.

This dish is so good, so simple, so delicate, that since I first tasted it at lunch in that Provençal inn I have cooked it scores of times, in the quantities given and also on a larger scale. It makes a lovely and easy dish for the type of menu on which it figured the day I first tasted it. The meal consisted of a typical Provençal hors d'oeuvre – pâté, tomato salad, olives, a few slices of sausage –

then the courgette gratin, followed by a daube of beef[1] served sizzling hot in a casserole brought to the table and left on it so that we could help ourselves. Then, as an alternative to the fruit, pastry, or crème caramel one would expect at the end of such a meal, we were offered a most delicious jam, home-made from green melons. There was no vegetable of any kind with the beef stew. We had good bread with which to mop up the juices, and that was enough.

ELIZABETH DAVID

Wine language

Perpetual nosing after snobbery at least suggests the snob.
Snob – A judge of merit by externals.
Wine Snob – A man or woman who drinks the label and the price.

It was in 1967 that my firm received the following advice, written on one of our pre-paid order cards, 'Why don't you wine snobs just drop dead – thank God for Tizer'. Unfortunately the writer failed to sign the card, which prevented me from sending him the following fictitious descriptions of a red and white wine to test his sense of humour. The first was made up by my friend Gerald Asher and the second by myself, and we still laugh at our expertise!

Ch. La Grave Trigant de Boisset, Premier Cru Pomerol, 1955. 'Deep colour and big shaggy nose. Rather a jumbly, untidy sort of wine with fruitiness shooting off one way, firmness another and body pushing around underneath' – if, that is, the pushing body hasn't squashed the shaggy nose in fruity jumble first!

Pouilly Blanc Fumé, Les Berthiers, 1966. 'Scintillating but deceptive colour, thin restless mini-skirted body which will develop into a seductive, generous and hedonistic wine "avec beaucoup du chien"; it will be more silky and appetizing than the 1964 vintage, a wine "qui s'allonge" – a wine with long legs? – if, that is, the long-legged body hasn't squeezed the finely chiselled nose out of its classic shape first!'

[1] For a recipe, with explanation, see Elizabeth David's 'French Provincial Cooking.'—Ed.

In point of fact the red wine was a typical Pomerol, full bodied but supple and velvety, and the Pouilly Blanc Fumé combined great elegance and breeding with bite and flinty flavour. To further illustrate the point of this article here are two true stories. Recently, at the Chelsea Flower Show, I overheard an old lady say to her companion, 'I like Lady Mohr. What a pity she has got such a dirty beard', and in Bordeaux a wine taster observe, 'What a pity Ch. Larosefleur has got such a tight little nose.' Which only goes to show that if you are a critic and lover of flowers or wine you develop your own descriptive language; being a lover of both I immediately knew what they were getting at!

Wine tasters have their own professional jargon which may at first sound affected, absurd or even pretentious, but when you come to learn it, it does make sense, and moreover the opinions of wine tasters achieve a higher label of unanimity than do the critics of music or literature.

At a blind tasting of young red table wines under 15s. od. the bottle, my old friend Harry Waugh showed me his first quick impression of one wine; under Taste he had scribbled 'communion wine'. The description exactly fitted my own impression, although my own thoughts had only got as far as a 'fat and unctuous, probably from Tarragona'.

And here you may be interested to read the descriptive language of William Mann, music critic of *The Times*, describing the quality of Thomas Hemsley's voice: 'His voice has its own timbre, nothing like Fischer-Dieskau's, more nasal, less rich, but very warm and forward, strong and varied in colour without a trace of flabbiness, an ideal instrument for the projection of words as music . . .' Full marks to William Mann, I say.

However, I digress. Of our five senses, taste and smell are, in general, the most neglected, and they have no permanent written language or record. I should add the words 'until now', because Michael Broadbent has recently compiled a wholly admirable glossary of tasting terms in the appendix to his book *Wine Tasting*. I strongly recommend you to study these conventional terms, which are used, by both professional and amateur wine tasters, to define their tastes and smells, so that they can be understood by other equally well-informed persons.

October

Wonderful downpour of leaf: when the morning
sun began to melt the frost, they fell at one touch
and in a few minutes a whole tree was flung of
them; they lay masking and papering the ground
at the foot. Then the tree seems to be looking down
on its cast self as blue sky on snow after a long fall,
its losing, its doing.

GERARD MANLEY HOPKINS 1873

E.N.T.

In Harley Street the initials E.N.T. stand for Ear, Nose and Throat; but in Jermyn Street we call them Eye, Nose and Taste.

If you were forced to accept, today, a sentence for the rest of your life of total blindness or total deafness, which would you choose? The question for all of us, who are neither blind nor deaf, is hypothetical but none the less agonizing and difficult to answer. My question has been put to a variety of friends and acquaintances, and their answers and the reasons for their choice have naturally varied according to their ages and the circumstances of their lives. For myself I would choose to be blind because the total loss of the sound of music and audible communication with those I love would place me into a world of loneliness for which sight could never compensate.

However, to those of us who are fortunate enough to retain all our senses it is the combination of Eye, Nose and Taste which gives us the maximum enjoyment of wine, and, to employ all three to the full, there are three golden aids to observe: the glass, the temperature of the wine, and decanting.[1]

The glass

I have drunk wine from glasses of all shapes, sizes, colour and thickness and I can assure you that it is not a 'mystique' of the Wine Trade when I say that the wrong type of glass can ruin the appreciation of a fine bottle of wine, and the right kind of glass can enhance beyond recognition the enjoyment of a 'vin ordinaire'.

A wine glass should be thin and large enough to hold a reasonable quantity of wine without filling it more than two thirds full, and it should be tulip shaped with a stem long enough to be held

[1] For Hints on Decanting, see page 161.

comfortably by the thumb and two fingers. A glass that conforms to this size and shape will enable you to tilt the wine to enjoy its colour without spilling. Its shape and stem will allow you to gently rotate the wine so that the bouquet is properly presented to your nose. Its width will ensure a broad stream of wine to be taken in directly to the sensitive sides of the mouth for you to savour its taste.

01-930 5557 = Christopher's

As yet a child, nor yet a fool to fame
I lisped in numbers, for the numbers came.
ALEXANDER POPE

Now that I am no longer a child, my remarkable memory – though I say it myself – for the exchange names and numbers of the leading Wine Shippers in London is no longer of any use to me. Gone are the days when London Wall 1878 meant Graham's Port, Whitehall 1810 Bollinger Champagne and Mansion House 5555 fine German wines. I cannot even transpose WHI into 944 because it is now 930. Even my beloved Kensington is 589 instead of 536; so for me KEN = 589 = LUX – which I can remember because I wash my socks in Lux and occasionally listen to Radio Luxemburg in the still hours of the night. The Grand Duchy of Luxemburg = 010 352 and the charge is 2d. for 3·75 seconds!

All the Old Faithfuls, which even a lisping child could remember, are gone. DIR is now 192, TIM = 123, ENG = 151, WEA = 246 8091. Only UMP remains untouched for the Test score at the Oval, providing of course that 246 8091 has not interrupted play! As for the recipes which we send you, why do we bother, when all you have to do is to dial 246 8071. But be careful, if your eyesight is as bad as mine, that you don't get 'The Main Events in and around London' – in Spanish!

Alas, as yet a fool to fame, the numbers do not come to me. So it is with a heavy heart that I say farewell to AMBassador – BAYswater – CHAncery – DRYden – EMPress – FLAXman – GROsvenor – HOLborn – IVAnhoe – JUNiper – KIPling – LANgham – MAYfair – NATional – OTTershaw – PADdington – RODney – SLOane – TRAfalgar – UNDerhill – VICtoria and WATerloo.

1966 MOSEL AND SAAR WINES

DHRONHOFBERGER SPÄTLESE, Mosel, *Geschwister Feilen*	19/6
GEIERSLAYER SONNSEITE SPÄTLESE, Mosel	22/6
Adolph Huesgen – Bocking.	
GRAACHER HIMMELREICH SPÄTLESE, Mosel, *Steffini*	23/–
DOM–SCHARZHOFBERGER, Saar, *Hohe Domkirche – Trier*	22/6
DOM–AVELSBACHER ALTENBERG, Saar	24/–
Hohe Domkirche – Trier	
SCHARZBERGER FEINE SPÄTLESE, Saar	25/–
Bernard Van Volxem – Wiltingen	

Here, at any rate, are some names that will never be replaced by numbers, except that of the cask from which they have been bottled.

October 1967

More change, less decay?

Plus ça change, plus c'est la même chose should be exactly true of the perfectly evolved type. The types which 'go under' are either those which do not know how to change, or do not know how to be '*la même chose*' under the variations. Many of you will remember Georgia Brown's talent in Lionel Bart's *Oliver!* and some of you have watched, and shared with her sharp and wistful eyes, her affectionate memories of London's East End in BBC2's very watchable series 'One Pair of Eyes'.

'*Chacun à son goût!*' Maybe *Oliver!* was not a musical to your taste and maybe you did not see Georgia Brown in 'One Pair of Eyes', in which case you have missed a personality with a rare gift. However, this old French proverb signifies for me, in my role of wine merchant and cook, a different kind of taste and variety of changes more sensual than philosophical.

In Mary McCarthy's novel *The Group* (was it to your taste?) they invented a competition for the most revolting dish of food which, if I remember rightly, resulted in two cold fried eggs with chocolate sauce and a glass of Crème de Menthe! I am not suggesting any such drastic changes in your diet, but would emphasize the word 'change' in our often hide-bound taste, both solid and liquid.

154

An October Dinner

Winter is nearly upon us and there is little to look forward to until the spring, except perhaps the delights of the table. My main course therefore is one which will give you a glimpse of the gourmet's paradise and leave happy memories to lighten the dull days ahead. It is however slightly expensive. We must, therefore, choose a setting for the chef d'oeuvre which, though fitting, is not costly.

SARDINES

Take four tinned sardines per person and roll them gently and carefully in seasoned flour. Dip in beaten egg and then into fine breadcrumbs. Repeat the egg and crumb process if necessary. Leave until the protective coating of crumbs is quite dry and when the time comes for frying they will require just two minutes in deep hot fat. Serve with a crisp lettuce leaf and slice or two of tomato with thin brown bread and butter and wedge of lemon. Don't waste time making sauce tartare: it is not an improvement!

PARTRIDGE

Bag, beg or poach one young partridge per person. Wipe the birds carefully with a cloth, season with pepper and salt and a squeeze of lemon juice and then roast them rare in butter. Take a thick slice of bread per person and fry in butter till crisp, arrange them on a serving dish and keep hot. Now in the same butter, with more added if necessary, gently fry thin slices of peeled and cored apple, enough to cover all the croûtons, and when just tender lay it evenly on top of them. Increase the heat of the pan and fry the birds quickly, again in added butter if necessary, turning them from time to time. This process will take no more than three to four minutes. Add to the pan a large glass of Calvados, allow it to flare, turning the birds in it all the time and when the flames have died down arrange the birds on top of the apple.

In the same pan, with all the juices that are left in it, make a sauce. Add (for four people) $\frac{1}{2}$ pint of dairy cream and salt and pepper to taste. Stir until the cream thickens. Add the juice of half a lemon, stir well and pour over the partridges.

ORANGE BOX SWEET

One packet sponge cakes, 1 pint of milk, two eggs, 1 desertspoonful gelatine, sugar to taste – about 2 oz. – two oranges, whipped
cream, chopped nuts, angelica, etc, and one plastic box with lid –
about 8 inches × 4 inches × 4 inches.

This is a most spectacular and easy-to-make dessert. Line the
box with sponge cakes sliced in half. Into a double saucepan put
the milk, beaten egg yolks, sugar, gelatine and the grated outer
rind of the oranges. Cook gently, until a thick custard has formed.
Add the orange juice and stir well in. Fold in the stiffly whipped
egg whites. Pour the mixture into the box and place the remaining
sponge cakes on top, then replace the lid firmly, leave in a ool
place. When quite set turn out on to a serving dish. Cover all over
with whipped cream, either with a stippled effect or smoothly
with piped decoration added. Then decorate generously with
chopped nuts, cherries.

LESLIE HOARE

Game

It is hard to think of October without thinking in terms of game;
they seem the ideal compromise between the fishes and chickens
of summer and the roasts and stews of winter months. My favourite game birds are pheasant and grouse; those young enough to
roast are so expensive that I buy them rarely, hoping for the
occasional present. Failing this, I often fall back on quail, which
are in fact now bred domestically and are therefore obtainable all
the year round. But they have the true gamey taste one yearns for.
They are also unusual enough to please guests who suffer from a
surplus of game, as they are not widely available. They can be
bought at Harrods and Fortnum & Mason. Most people allow
two birds per person, but if they form part of a fairly substantial
meal, one can suffice. After many experiments, I believe the
following is the best way to cook them:

ROAST QUAIL

For six quail: Bring a large saucepan of milk to boiling point.
Drop in the birds, and allow seven minutes from the moment the
milk comes back to simmering point. Lift out each bird and dry

carefully in a cloth. Impale them on a spit and pour a little melted butter over each one. (You will have to do them in two batches, being careful to keep the first ones hot.) Roast for eight minutes Failing a spit, roast them in a fairly quick oven (gas No. 5, 375°F), for the same time.

They can be served in a variety of ways, according to the nature of the meal. For a light, elegant dish – perhaps for a supper after the theatre, they can be laid on a dish of grapes or sweet corn, previously heated in the oven, with their juices poured over them. A platter of wild rice also makes a delicious but extravagent bed on which to lay them. For a more filling and economical meal they can be served on a risotto, which also makes a good accompaniment to other game birds.

RISOTTO

For six: Melt 4 oz. butter in a heavy saucepan and cook a large, finely chopped onion in it until golden. Add 1 breakfast cupful ($\frac{1}{2}$ pint) round Italian rice and stir around for a few minutes until it is almost transparent. Have 3 pints chicken or beef stock heated until almost boiling, and add it to the rice, 1 cupful at a time, stirring occasionally, until each one is absorbed. By the time all the stock is used up, the rice should be tender; the whole operation will take about thirty minutes. Pour on to the serving dish, lay the quails on top and pour their juices over. (If cooking for three, allowing two quails each, use a teacup instead of a breakfast cup and halve the other quantities.)

ARABELLA BOXER

. . . more game

'There is a good deal more dispute as to the time, or in other words the degree, to which grouse ought to be roasted than in regard to most other game – there is a school who would have grouse decidely underdone. I think they are wrong – there should be nothing in the very least saignant about a grouse when he is carved – if possible he should be taken away from the fire the very minute that the last possibility of such a trace has disappeared.'

Thus George Saintsbury on the cookery of grouse in the *Fur, Feather and Fin* series of volumes published in the 1890's by Longmans Green, and directed mainly at amateur naturalists and sportsmen.

Professor Saintsbury, who knew little of the technicalities of cookery but held decided views which make him always entertaining and sometimes infuriating, provided his readers with a treatise on the eating of grouse rather than on its cookery. He detested what he claimed was the Scottish custom of serving melted butter sauce with grouse and approved Soyer's declaration that nothing but a crust of bread should form the solid accompaniment to the bird. The renowned chef's uncharacteristic restraint in this matter is quickly nullified by his suggestion that 'a little sweet champagne' will go nicely with the bird. Having disposed of this scandalous heresy, 'spoken like a Frenchman', the Professor goes on without the bat of an eyelid to assert that 'second growth clarets – Cos d'Estournel or Durfort' are the proper wines for grouse. Burgundy he will allow, so long as it is not the best – a crumb, if not a crust, of comfort for some of us.

ROAST GROUSE

The most prudent course is to weigh each bird, to put a lump of butter inside each, wrap them separately in a piece of well-buttered paper, pack them closely on their sides in an appropriate-sized roasting tin and give them, whatever their weight, a basic twenty-five minutes (turning them over at half time) at a temperature of 410–30°F, or gas No. 6–7.

After the first twenty-five minutes, unwrap the birds, put them back in the oven and, treating each bird individually, allow an extra two minutes for every ounce over 10 oz., meaning that a grouse of 15 oz. weight takes thirty-five minutes to cook. This sounds a long time (authorities, and there are many of them, who give fifteen minutes as the roasting time for grouse and partridge must have ovens very different from mine. Or perhaps they have different clocks) but should produce a fully grown, mid-season bird cooked just enough to remain delicately pink with no trace of rawness.

Professor Saintsbury advocates watercress with grouse; he does not care for gravy, observes that 'breadcrumbs unless very well cooked are the reverse of appetizing', and calls attention to the super-excellence of the cold roast bird in the severest simplicity.

To me, a plain cold grouse or partridge is better than a hot one (unless it has been spit-roasted), always provided that it is eaten on the day or the day after it has been cooked, and cooled naturally, not chilled in the refrigerator.

POTTED GAME

Grouse 'potted whole, stowed singly into pots with clarified butter poured over' as described by Professor Saintsbury (the old boy didn't miss much) are infinitely enticing, exceedingly extravagant with butter and not very practical for these days. But you can make one young cooked grouse or partridge go a very long way by the simple method of chopping the flesh, freed from all skin and sinew with about one quarter of its weight in mild, rather fat, cooked ham. You then put the chopped grouse and ham in the electric blender with 4 tablespoonfuls of clarified butter to every $\frac{1}{2}$ lb. of the mixture. Add salt if necessary, a few grains of cayenne, a few drops of lemon juice, reduce the mixture to a paste or purée. Pack it in to small straight-sided china, glazed earthenware or glass pots. Put these into the refrigerator until the meat is very cold and firm. Then seal the pots with a layer of just-melted clarified butter.

Potted game is most delicate and delicious with hot thin crisp brown toast for tea or as a first course at lunch.

It goes without saying that old birds can, equally, be used for potting, but they are much less delicate, need very long slow and thorough cooking, a larger proportion of fat ham (or pickled pork but not smoked bacon), and must be carefully drained of their cooking juices before they are prepared for chopping and pounding, otherwise sediment seeps through, collects at the bottom of the little jars and causes mould.

ELIZABETH DAVID

The Noble Cabbage

Cookery writers get in grooves, writing of turkey in December, primeurs in the spring, ices and cups in the summer, and of game in October. This October, like a tram given the freedom of a trolley-bus, I shall write in praise of cabbage.

Cabbage soup – by whatever French regional name – is a thing of beauty. Usually you begin by sweating, as it is unattractively called, potatoes, carrots and leeks in butter or pork fat. Then you add stock or the liquid in which you have cooked a gammon. When the vegetables are cooked and seasoned, add cabbage cut in strips and cook until it is tender. No thickening is required, if you have used enough vegetables, and no poshing-up with egg-yolks and cream: it is a country soup.

Cabbage can appear in hors d'oeuvre in two forms: stuffed or as cole slaw. Stuffed cabbage as a main dish needs to be larger: for hors d'oeuvre it should be the size of Greek dolmas, stuffed vine leaves. In either case you make a stuffing with cooked lamb, beef or chicken – plus rice, if you like – with plenty of herbs and spices: wrap the leaves (several if thin) round the stuffing, tie them with cotton and cook them in a buttered fireproof dish with a little stock. Cut off the cotton before serving. Some like a tomato sauce. I don't. When cold, as hors d'ocuvre, I like pieces of lemon to squeeze on. If you want to be very Greek, make an avgolemono sauce with lemons and egg-yolk.

Cole slaw is simply white cabbage, cut julienne very finely and mixed with mayonnaise and cream. Extra pepper or mustard is a matter of taste. It is good in a mixed hors d'oeuvre, excellent as a salad with cold meat and wonderful (on a separate cold plate) with hot roast beef.

Cabbage as a vegetable is a horror if soggy and overcooked. I cut a white cabbage very fine, wash it in a colander and add no water to that which remains on it. I cook it over a low flame adding salt and pepper, till it is cooked but still firm. It takes only about five minutes. Then I drain off the water through the colander, put a lump of butter in the saucepan and put back the cabbage to steam off the rest of the water. At this point I stir in a tablespoonful of wine vinegar and a tablespoonful of apricot jam.

Good but quite different is bubble-and-squeak: boiled potato and cooked green cabbage, mashed together and cooked like a thick pancake in dripping or butter in a heavy saucepan, turned at half time to brown on both sides.

ROBIN MCDOUALL

Hints on Decanting

I have three friends coming to lunch on Saturday and I propose to give them a dish of scallops with a bottle of Traminer 1964, followed by roast lamb and cheese, when we will drink Ch. Les Petits Arnauds, Blaye 1962 and Ch. Haut Bages Liberal, Pauillac 1952.

Here is how I propose to deal with the two red wines. Firstly I must remember to take the two bottles gently out of their bin or rack on Friday and stand them upright in an even temperature for about twenty-four hours. As I am both cook and butler, I must work to a plan and see that my tools for the operation are ready in advance. I will require two decanters; personally I use plain Swedish crystal decanters costing about 65s. od. But it is quite in order to decant your wine into another clean bottle of the same size – a white Sauternes bottle will do very well. I shall also need a sharp knife, a clean moist rag (no detergents please!), a corkscrew of the cantilever type – the screw itself must be rounded and not one of those with sharp edges – a large funnel of glass, enamel or plastic (but not one of those mini-skirted things one sees!) and last, but not least, a candle in a stick, or a torch which will stand on its end.

At 11 am on Saturday, I am ready to decant the 1962 bottle, because its youth will benefit from the stimulus of fresh oxygen for two hours. I now check that my decanter is clean and sweet, and that it is about the same temperature as my bottle of wine – a small but important point. If the decanter is very cold, rinse it out with tepid water and then get rid of every drop. Place the funnel in the bottle and put it on a table of average height, with the candle or torch to the right and below the level of the rim of the funnel.

Now I am ready to deal with the bottle. It has been standing up for twenty-four hours, so all the sediment is lodged in the narrow space at the bottom of the bottle between the punt and the side of the bottle. With a sharp knife, I cut off the capsule below the lip of the neck, so that when I pour the wine into the decanter it will not come in contact with the lead of the capsule. With my moist, clean rag I remove any encrustation which has formed round the cork and the lip of the bottle. The cantilever action of my cork-screw enables me to draw the cork smoothly and gradually without any violent jerk.

Now for the operation itself. It does require a steady hand and a dark room. So light the candle or torch, and draw the curtains. Personally, I use a torch, because heavy breathing is apt to make the candle flicker! So, fear nothing! and grasp the bottle firmly in your right hand (unless you are left handed!) towards the bottom of the bottle, and using the index finger of your left hand as a support under the neck of the bottle, tilt the mouth of the bottle over the rim of the funnel and begin to pour. At this stage it is most important to pour continuously, steadily and slowly. Your head is now over the shoulder of the bottle and the light of the candle or torch shining through the bottle will give you a clear view of the wine. The position and height of the candle or torch relative to the rim of your funnel and the shoulder of the bottle can easily be judged by sighting an empty bottle over the light. The wine should pour out of the bottle steadily and slowly without the slightest glugging sound. As the bottle reaches the horizontal position pour a little faster and watch carefully for the first sign of the dark streak of the deposit which will emerge slowly from under your right hand. When this streak reaches the end of the neck of the bottle stop pouring, and you will be amazed that you have only lost a sherry glass of wine.

For your own satisfaction, pour the dregs into a glass and compare its taste with the bright and perfect wine in the decanter.

I shall decant the 1952 wine an hour later. It is impossible to lay down exact rules for how long a wine should be decanted before drinking, as it depends so much on the character and degree of maturity of the wine. For young robust wines about two hours is a safe guide, while for older and more delicate wine about one hour will be enough.

Very young 'vins ordinaires' will be greatly improved by decanting four or five hours before you drink them and will reveal qualities that would take some years in bottle to acquire. You will be surprised how much better they will taste.

Lastly, if due to short notice, you are unable to stand your bottle upright for twenty-four hours, all you have to do is take the bottle very carefully and slowly from the bin or wine rack and move it in its horizontal position into a bottle basket. With the bottle in this basket, remove the capsule and draw the cork. Then lift the bottle out of the basket very carefully, and still in its recumbent position, and pour it straight away into your decanter in the manner already described.

November

. . . it has been a common notion among heedless observers that the robin frequents no were but in villages but this is an erronious one for it is found in the deepest solitudes of woods and forrests were it lives on insects and builds its nest on the roots or stools of the underwood or under a hanging bank by a dykeside which is often mistook for that of the nightingales. I have often observed its fondness for man even here for in summer I scarcely cross a wood but a Robin suddenly falls in my path to court my acquaintance and pay me a visit were it hops and flutters about as if pleased to see me and in winter it is the woodman's companion for the whole day and the whole season who considers it as his neighbour and friend.

JOHN CLARE 1825

Tawny Port

'Wine that is saleable and good needeth no bush or garland of Yew to be hanged before.'
RICHARD TAVERNER, 1539 *Proverbs.*

Not everyone knows the virtues of Tawny Port. Those who dismiss port as being too heavy a drink for them might find in fine old Tawny Port a revelation. All red port when it is made is a big, full-bodied, purple-red wine. If it is matured in wood, it gradually loses body and colour. After a few years it becomes fit for drinking and much of it then is sold for Ruby Port. But some of the finest is allowed to go on maturing for many years more and develops into Tawny Port. It is now no longer the 'Stout Fruity' of its earliest days, and, though it still retains most of its strength, its youthful corpulence and complexion have fined down into a fragrant and delicate elegance and a soft red-golden hue. Fine Tawny Port is a delightful drink at any time of day. In warm weather, chilled, it is nectar. Real Tawny Port can never be cheap. It was fine wine to start with, to last so long, and it has had many years, sometimes several decades, of care. Fine Tawny Port is tawny with age, and it is delicious.

Wine, Insomnia and Song

Ah, make the most of what we yet may spend,
Before we too into Dust Descend;
Dust into Dust, and under Dust, lie,
Sans Wine, Sans Song, Sans Singer, and – Sans End.
EDWARD FITZGERALD, 1809–83

While lying in bed, with a rather irritable bed companion Insomnia, at an RAC & AA recommended hotel in Salisbury, (no bedside lamp, one powerful bulb in a minute shade suspended from the centre of ceiling, light switch ten feet away by the door), a consoling thought came to my rescue!

On the 29th October, at 8 pm one song cycle should suffice to fill the Festival Hall, and there are not many songs that can boast of such a record! Admittedly it has the musical genius of Ludwig van Beethoven, assisted by the world's most beautiful baritone voice of Dietrich Fischer-Dieskau and by that incomparable accompanist, Gerald Moore, on the piano and, of course, the audience of which I hope to be a part.

'What has all this got to do with Wine?' you may say. My answer is that, if Neville Cardus can write for the *Guardian* on music and cricket, then surely I may touch on music and wine for Christopher's – because, after Beethoven's miraculous song, I propose with my companion of the evening to drink a bottle of Moselle, a wine much beloved of Beethoven.

Like the song, ('An die ferne Geliebte' Opus 98, 1816), the wine, (Maximin Gruenhaeuser Herrenberg 1964. Growth Carl von Schubert (sic.)), is something of a miracle, and also requires three things to complete its nobility of bouquet and flavour – the loving care and skill of its 'growers', the quality and balance of its grapes and the blessings of Nature, and thirdly the devotion and enthusiasm of its consumer. The Moselle wines of the year 1964 are the best I have tasted in thirty years.

We have bought six wonderful Moselle wines of the year 1964.

OBEREMMELER SCHARZBERG SPÄTLESE	18/6
KANZEMER ALTENBERG, NATURREIN	22/6
EITELSBACHER SONNENBERG RIESLING SPÄTLESE	25/6
WILTINGER SCHLANGENGRABEN-RÖMERBRUNNEN SPÄTLESE	25/6
MAXIMIN GRUENHAEUSER HERRENBERG	30/6
BERNKASTELER GRABEN FEINE AUSLESE	37/6

November 1965

Few principles, no loyalties?

'The arrogance of age must submit to be taught by youth.'
EDMUND BURKE, Letter to Fanny Burney, 1782

Included in a book called *The New London Spy – A discreet guide to the City's pleasures* (Anthony Blond 30s. od.), there is a savage attack on London Society, the Enclave or the Establishment, depending on what you like to call it. In this attack, dripping with vitriol, the anonymous author tells me that one of the qualifications for membership of this Society, if I am not already born into it, is to be a supremely arrogant wine merchant with few principles and no loyalties except to the Enclave and all it stands for.

I wonder why the anonymous author picked on the wine merchant for the qualifications of supreme arrogance, let alone one with few principles and no loyalties. When I first joined Christopher's I can remember, to my shame, a certain sense of superiority over my friends engendered by the first heady draughts from the vast vats of wine knowledge. Since those far off days of ignorance I know that arrogance and wine will never make a palatable blend, and will only lead to ridicule and contempt. A lack of principle and loyalty will lose you not only your customer but the man from whom you buy your wine. Part of the pleasure of a wine merchant is the camaraderie of our trade, and the trust we place in each other. Each day I discover and learn from some new facet, however small, of the many coloured jewel that is wine.

All this leads me to tell you that Jacques Calvet is a man that I honour, more than most in the Wine Trade, for his sincerity and complete lack of conceit. My heart goes out to him and the House of Calvet in the recent disaster by fire that they have suffered in Bordeaux. I have never heard him speak arrogantly of wine, nor make a snide remark about his competitors. It is thanks to his integrity and that of his forebears that the wines of Calvet bear the unique honour and title of Diplôme du Prestige de la France. I wish the House of Calvet a speedy recovery from the cruel blow that has struck them.

November 1966

The Food for November

LA POULE AU POT DU BÉARNAIS

This is just one version of this celebrated method of cooking a good fat boiling chicken. A large, deep saucepan or earthenware pot is essential so that there is plenty of room for a variety of vegetables and a good covering of water, or the broth will boil away and its goodness be lost.

The chicken is stuffed with a mixture of the pounded liver of the bird, a good handful of breadcrumbs soaked in milk and squeezed dry, ¼ lb. of chopped or minced fresh pork, and parsley and seasoning, into which you stir an egg or two. Brown the chicken all over in good dripping or butter add six carrots, a small turnip, two onions, a couple of sliced leeks, a piece of celery and salt. Pour in boiling water to cover the bird and the vegetables, and when the water comes to the boil again remove any scum which rises to the top. Cover the pan and simmer very slowly for about three hours. Forty-five minutes or so before serving, the vegetables, which have been cooking in the pot and which, by now, are rather sodden and tasteless, can be removed and fresh ones added.

Serve the chicken with the vegetables all round and a sauce vinaigrette slightly thickened with egg yolks, as described below. The broth is best kept as a basis for soup for another meal.

SAUCE VINAIGRETTE WITH EGG YOLKS

Chop a couple of shallots or tiny onions with 2 tablespoonfuls of parsley and any other fresh herbs you may have, such as tarragon, chervil, chives. Season with salt, freshly milled pepper and a teaspoonful of yellow French mustard. Stir gradually, 4–6 tablespoonfuls of mild olive oil, and a couple of teaspoonfuls of tarragon vinegar.

QUINCES AND WINE

In Greece, in South Western France and in certain parts of Spain it is appreciated that quince sweetmeats make one of the most admirable of all companions for the local dessert wines, the Muscats of Lunel, the golden wine of Monbazillac, the Malmsey or Monemvasia of the Greeks and the Monovar of the province of Alicante.

Spanish quince paste or cheese can be bought in Soho shops (try King Bomba's Italian Produce Stores, 37 Old Compton Street, W1) and there are now some admirable English quince conserves on the market. One of these comes from the Elsenham Jam Company of Essex, another is made by a Sussex firm called

169

Dorothy Carter, at Rye, and is obtainable from the Empire Shop, 42 Sloane Street, SW1.

Eaten with cream or with fresh cream cheese, these conserves make a delicious dessert for the midday meal. The addition of a spoonful or two of quince conserve or jelly to apple tarts, pies and charlottes is a traditional piece of English country kitchen lore well worth reviving. The quince gives a scent and a flavour to the apples which lifts them from banality more subtly and more effectively than the customary lemon or spices.

For those who have their own quinces, or can buy, or beg them from those who don't like them or cannot be bothered with them, a quince compote is a simple recipe.

ELIZABETH DAVID

A Meatless Dinner

I think one of the hardest things to think up is a good but unpretentious dinner to give to Catholics on a Friday. One can't always afford salmon or sole, many people don't eat shellfish, and one hasn't the gall to do plaice and chips, delicious though they are. This whole meal can be done well in advance, reheated, or even kept hot.

SOUPE AUX POSSIONS

For six people: about 1 lb. fishheads, bones and skin, 1 lb. fresh haddock, hake, cod, whiting or mullet or a mixture of these, four tomatoes, one clove garlic, one chicken stock cube, 1 tablespoonful tomato purée, ½ oz. butter, a large bunch of parsley, one bay-leaf, a pinch of thyme, one onion, black pepper, 2 oz. peeled prawns if liked, three small slices white bread and a little olive oil.

Put the fishheads, skins and bones into a large saucepan with half the parsley, half the onion and the bayleaf. Cover with water and simmer for twenty minutes. Strain and throw away the bones. Now chop the second half of the onion very finely, and cook gently in the butter in a large saucepan. When the onion is soft and translucent, pour on the fish stock and add the tomato purée, the garlic (crushed), the chicken stock cube, the thyme, and plenty of ground black pepper, Be wary of adding salt as the stock cube is salty. Bring to the boil, add the fish cut into 1-inch cubes, taking care to remove any bones. Cover the pan and simmer very gently for fifteen minutes. Plunge the tomatoes into boiling water for five seconds, remove and skin them. Slice them thickly, chop the rest of the parsley. Cut the crusts off the bread, quarter the slices diagonally, and fry the triangles slowly in the olive oil until golden. Just before serving add the sliced tomatoes and the prawns to the soup and reheat. Dip the crôutons into the chopped parsley and serve with the soup.

CHOUFLEUR A LA POLONAISE

One cauliflower, cut into fleurets and boiled in salted water until just tender, butter, the yolks of four hardboiled eggs, 1 heaped tablespoonful white breadcrumbs, 1 tablespoonful chopped parsley, four tomatoes, skinned and chopped, a small onion, chopped.

Gently fry the cauliflower in an ounce of butter until brown on all sides, take the pieces out and re-form into a cauliflower shape on the serving dish. Put the onion into the frying pan with a little more butter, and cook gently until soft, add the tomato, cook two minutes more and pour over the cauliflower. Wipe out the pan, melt another ounce of butter and fry the crumbs until golden. Mix in the chopped yolks, and lastly the parsley. Scatter this over the cauliflower and season well with salt and ground black pepper.

To make perfect sauté potatoes, boil the potatoes in their skins, peel them, cut them up roughly, and fry until brown in a little butter with a pinch of ground rosemary.

For a salad, slice four small courgettes and boil them briefly in salted water. Cook $\frac{1}{4}$ lb. French beans cut in half, and boil a small packet of frozen sweetcorn. Slice four sticks of celery, and mix with the other ingredients. Dress with a good vinaigrette.

CRÈME BRULÉE

Four egg yolks, 1 tablespoonful sugar, 1 pint cream, vanilla essence, caster sugar for the top. Mix the yolks with the table-spoonful of sugar, in a deep bowl. Put the cream and a few drops of vanilla essence into a saucepan and bring to boiling point. Pour the hot cream on to the yolks, mixing well. Now place the bowl over a saucepan of boiling water so that the bottom of the bowl is just clear of the water. Stir constantly while the custard is thickening. It must not boil, but should just reach scalding point. Strain into a pie dish and allow to stand overnight. Put an even layer of caster sugar, about one fifth of an inch thick, on the surface of the cream and place under a very hot grill until the sugar has melted and turned brown. Cool completely before serving.

PRUDENCE LEITH

And talking of Calvet, here are two clarets we have recently bought from this famous old firm.

TAUZIA, St Émilion	18/7
CHATEAU SOCIANDO, Blaye 1962	15/10

Prices include Import Surcharge and Regulator Tax.
November 1966

Thoughts Occasioned by St Andrew's Day

Christian Isabel Johnstone, whose *Cook and Housewife's Manual* was published in 1827 under the pseudonym of Mistress Margaret Dods, was the wife of John Johnstone, a Dunfermline school-master who became editor and proprietor of the *Inverness Courier* and subsequently joint editor with his wife of the *Edinburgh Weekly Chronicle*. Mrs Johnstone took her pen name from Meg Dods, landlady of the Cleikum Inn in Auldtown of St Ronan's, a character created by Sir Walter Scott in *St. Ronan's Well*. There were indeed rumours, presumably not discouraged by Mrs John-stone's publishers, to the effect that the conversational footnotes to many of the recipes were contributed by Sir Walter himself. Nowadays these wordy notes make heavy reading. It is the recipes proper which interest us, so much so that a century and a half after its original publication the book is still a source of reference for cooks in search of traditional Scottish recipes for salmon, game birds and venison and for the old national dishes such as haggis, cock-a-leekie, sheep's head broth, Friar's chicken, oat cakes and cream cheeses.

On the salting, curing and smoking of meat and fish as practised in Scotland, Mrs Johnstone is particularly interesting. Notes on salted mutton and goose as well as on hams, beef, sausages and a 'Yule Mart or whole Bullock', figure in the *Cook's and Housewife's Manual*. 'Mutton, either ribs or breast, may be salted and served boiled with roots, making at the same time potato soup, seasoned with parsley or celery.' A dish called 'Collier's roast' was a leg of mutton salted for a week, roasted and served with mashed turnip or browned potatoes; in Caithness 'geese are cured and smoked and are highly relishing. Smoked solan geese are well known as contributing to the abundance of the Scottish breakfast'.

The Manual includes no detailed prescription for the salted and smoked goose, but Mrs Johnstone gives illuminating notes on the wood used for smoking, and the salt and spices then in common use for the curing of meats: 'green birch, oak, or the odoriferous woods, as juniper, etc, are an immense improvement to all dried meats. And no sort of meat', she adds, 'is more improved by smoking with aromatic woods than mutton'.

Although mutton has become a rather rare commodity a good butcher will always procure it to order (and given the formula, would possibly even be interested in trying the salting and spicing method), while halves of first-class year-old mutton or hogget, comprising separated leg, loin, and shoulder joints ready for cooking or for storage in the deep freeze can be ordered by post from a Norfolk breeder, Lord Fisher, of Kilverstone, Thetford, Norfolk. Minimum weight of the meat is 18 lb., price £6, dispatch is every Wednesday.

Here is the Meg Dods formula for pork or mutton hams, a recipe which is well worth a revival. Smoking of the hams is by no means essential, although it would be pleasant if some enterprising meat-curer would attempt the restoration of this ancient and excellent speciality.

TO CURE HAMS

'Choose the short, thick legs of clean-fed hogs. Those which are just old enough to have the flesh of firm texture, and which have roamed at large in a forest, are far the best.

'To each large ham allow ½ lb. of bay salt,[1] 2 oz. of saltpetre, 9 oz. of coarse sugar, and ½ lb. of common salt, with 4 oz. of Jamaica[2] and black pepper, and one of coriander seeds.

'Pound the ingredients and beat and mix them well; but first rub in about 6 oz. of the salt and the saltpetre and, after two days the rest of the salt and the spices. Rub for a long half-hour.

'Lay the hams in the trough; keep them carefully covered, and baste them with the brine every day. Turn them occasionally, and rub with the brine: make more brine if necessary.'

For a mutton ham, Mrs Johnstone prescribes a quarter the given quantity of salt and saltpetre, and half proportions of sugar and spices. Juniper berries (also used in the curing of the famous dry-spiced beef sold at Harrods) are recommened by Mrs Johnstone as being a characteristic Highland addition to the spice mixture for cured mutton. The proportion is approximately 1½ oz., roughly pounded, for one mutton ham. A week to ten days in the brine (which is produced by the sugar, salt and the meat itself) should be allowed for the mutton ham. Cooking is much as for pork hams, or gammon.

ELIZABETH DAVID

James Boswell

On my holiday I took with me *A Shorter Boswell* edited by John Bailey, author of *Dr. Johnson and his Circle*. This little book contains 195 extracts, short and long, from James Boswell's *Life of Doctor Samuel Johnson*, and it has prompted me to give you this excerpt

[1]Sea Salt
[2]Allspice or pimento berries

from a letter written by James Boswell, dated 17th August 1792, to *The Public Advertiser*.[1]

'Sir, As a sequel to the well-written letters in your paper against the absurd introduction of French phrases into our language, I send you the following pleasant copy of verses:

MR BOSWELL TO HIS WINE MERCHANT
What a Frenchified jargon is heard every day,
While good plain old English seems wearing away?
Should a Cit for fresh air out to Islington go,
His snug little box is forsooth his Château!
To build castles in th'air shou'd a schemer incline,
Parbleu, l'on bâtit des châteaux en Espagne –
Dear Edwards, there's one thing I certainly know;
The Château I love is your Château Margaux!'

Mr E. K. Willing-Denton of the Manor, Middlewich, Cheshire. kindly sent me this delightful verse and he tells me that, to the best of his knowledge and belief, this letter has not been reprinted since the date of the newspaper quoted above. Meanwhile we hope that one of our readers can give us the following information. Who was Boswell's wine merchant, and what is the earliest reference in the English language to an individual Château in the Médoc?

Madeira

It is to the marriage of Charles II with Catherine of Braganza that we owe our taste for the wines of Madeira. English merchants were attracted to this island, a gleaming gem in the crown of Portugal, because, by this marriage, they enjoyed preferential treatment. By 1680 there were ten British firms exporting wine, principally to the Colonies in America. The men, who spread the fame of Madeira wines throughout the world, include

[1] The paper started as *The Grand Adviser*, took over *The Covent Garden Journal* and became the *Public Advertiser* on 1st December 1752. Henry Sampson Woodfall became editor at the age of 19 in 1758 and Master of the Stationers' Company in 1797.

William Bolton, John Leacock and Francis Newton, and those in this century – who have carried on the tradition – Blandy, Gordon, Cossart, Power, Leacock, Miles and Rutherford, to mention but a few.

In 1772 Leacock shipped wine to John Carbonnell for George III. 'Agreeable to your desire we have shipt you by Capn James Young four butts of as fine wine as ever was exported from this island. It is three years old – has been to Brazil – pale colour – rich taste and nutt flavour – and if ever Madeira Wine pleased His Majesty this certainly must. They are part of our private stock, and, we aver to you, are not to be had here for any money. But to oblige you, and satisfy your pressing particular and repeated recommendation about them, we let you have them at £40 the regular pipe of 100 gallons. We repeat again you could not for any money obtain 4 butts more of such wine in all the Island. For, besides their age and being the round they are the growth of a particular spot of ground, the excellence of what it produces we have experienced for 20 years. We were very particular in repairing the casks, which are firmed with 12 iron hoops each![1]

In 1919 I had a school chum called Blandy, and my mother had a diamond brooch in the shape of three ostrich feathers with, underneath, the motto 'Ich Dien'. Blandy came from Madeira; my mother's brooch came from my step-father, who had the honour to command the 10th Royal Hussars.

ORDERS Adjutant-General's Office, 27 September 1783. It is His Majesty's pleasure that the Tenth Regiment of Light Dragoons shall in future be called the Tenth, or Prince of Wales's Own Regiment of Light Dragoons.[2]

'The three ostrich feathers are supposed to have been derived from the badge of Queen Philippa (the Mother of Edward the Black Prince), being the appanage of the eldest son of the House of Hainault.'[3]

---

[1] This quotation is taken, with acknowledgment and thanks, from Rupert Croft-Cooke's book *Madeira*. It is a fascinating story of this island's history, people and wine, and was originally published by Putnam.
[2] It was at this this time that they assumed the present badge and motto.
[3] Liddell, *Memoirs of Tenth Royal Hussars*, p. 59.

I like to think that George III was sipping a glass of his pale, rich nutty Madeira wine when it was his pleasure to bestow this honour on the 10th Light Dragoons. Now, fifty years after my first encounter with Blandy and 186 years since the 10th Royal Hussars first wore the three ostrich feathers as their badge, I hope and believe that the two pipes of Rare old Verdelho, which Christopher's have shipped to mark the Investiture of Prince Charles as Prince of Wales, is 'as fine a wine as was ever exported from this Island'.

Enamelled in gold into the bottle will be the heir apparent's emblem, together with the date of the Investiture. The label is gold blocked on a royal purple background. The wine is a collector's item, to be laid down, and drunk, at its best, on the 25th anniversary of the Investiture. All the bottles from sixty-one upwards – the Prince of Wales has accepted the first sixty – will be numbered, and there will be only a very limited quantity.

December

A plant of misseltoe grows on a bough of the medlar: it abounds
in my hedges on the maple. The air is full of insects. Turkies strut
and gobble. Many lambs at the Priory.

GILBERT WHITE 1780

December

To move house and, at the same time, welcome into one's new home an eight-week-old brindle Staffordshire Bull Terrier has been an exhausting but delightful experience. Bodger, or to give him his full name, Ashstock Brigadier Bodger, demands and gets non-stop love and attention from 6 am to his bedtime, none of which is exactly conducive to writing.

So, if my finale is somewhat rambling, I hope you will bear with me – especially since I am taking 'sabbatical leave' from composing and editing Christopher's *Wine and Food Leaflets*. It has been ten years since our first humble efforts appeared in print, and I want to thank all those friends, old and new, who have helped me so generously with its composition.

'Friends disappear with the dregs from the empty wine casks!
HORACE

Ever since I joined Christopher's in 1936 I can remember Arthur Whitworth, great crony of my old boss 'Annie' Irish. For me he has always been part and parcel of my old firm, both as customer and friend. And I am happy to tell you that he is a friend who has not disappeared with the dregs from any wine cask. In fact, this remarkable man, who looks not a day over seventy-five, is in his ninety-fourth year! He also bears the honourable title of 'Our Oldest Customer'.

Recently he sent me some lines he came across in one of E. V. Lucas's books, and he tells me that E.V. himself could not say who was the author. Here they are – perhaps you may be able to help us.

> *How brew the brave drink, Life?*
> *Take of the herb hight 'Morning Joy',*
> *Take of the herb hight 'Evening Rest',*
> *Pour in Pain lest Bliss should cloy, . .*
> *Shake in Sin to give it Zest,*
> *Then down with the brave drink, Life!*

Ten years as a regular soldier, four years a Prisoner of War and over thirty years in the Wine Trade have brought me into contact with a vast variety of fascinating people. It has been these countless opportunities to observe, talk with, and listen to people from all walks of life which have made my life so happy and interesting.

There is nothing like the retail wine trade to bring you into personal relationship with the public and to learn about their foibles, tastes and temperaments, whether they be choleric or gentle, generous or mean. Acceptance of genuine criticism, tolerance or understanding of peoples' beliefs and tastes other than your own seldom meet with complete failure in communication. I believe that communication is one of the essences of human relationship. I only wish that we could gather some of the power-corrupted politicians of the world round a wine merchant's dinner table and get them to communicate with each other under the influence of good food and wine! Alas! without a sense of humour, communication is often powerless to do good.

I remember receiving a telephone call from a highly respected Covent Garden Merchant at about 5 pm, a few days before Christmas. I was tired and irritable and the conversation ran as follows: could we deliver to them some wine for luncheon the next day? 'My dear sir, don't you realise it is the height of the Christmas rush, I doubt if any firm in London could do this at such short notice – do you mean to tell me that you could deliver a ton of potatoes to us tomorrow morning?!' 'Yes,' came the answer, 'we certainly could and we will dump them on the pavement outside your door at 8 am!' Pause – followed by hilarious laughter at both ends of the line. They got their wine by taxi and we were spared the potatoes!

There is no trade in the world where there exists so much goodwill, generosity, mutual trust and integrity as in the Wine Trade. For the little I know about wine, I am indebted to my friends in our honourable trade. I thank them all for their wise counsel and for the memorable bottles we have shared. May they prosper and enjoy good health and peace in the years ahead.

Now that I have a small house in a tiny plot of garden, a wonderful wife and a Staffordshire bull terrier with a taste for black olives, what more can a man want – except to wish you all a Happy New Year!

A December Menu

TURTLE CONSOMMÉ

For six people, three tins of turtle consommé; one large sherry glass of Sercial madeira or medium sherry, a lemon.

Since this menu is designed as a simplified meal for Christmas or New Year entertaining on a small scale it starts off with something which needs no cooking at all – hot turtle consommé into which, when it is heated, you pour madeira or sherry, and a squeeze of lemon juice.

Turtle consommé is very rich, and one cup per person is usually enough. Dry crisp brown toast is welcome with the consommé, and so on the table is something for people to nibble while the bird is being carved: salted almonds, Spanish green olives stuffed with anchovies, or the delicious little Japanese cocktail biscuits which most good grocers stock at Christmas time.

ROAST TURKEY WITH PARSLEY AND LEMON STUFFING

One 10–14 lb. turkey (dressed and drawn weight).

For the stuffing: ½ lb. dried breadcrumbs; two large lemons; 6 tablespoonfuls of finely chopped parsley; ½ lb. unsalted butter; three whole eggs; salt, freshly milled pepper.

For cooking the turkey: butter; cooking foil; small metal skewers; large baking tin and rack.

To prepare the breadcrumbs for the stuffing, cut the crusts from a sliced white loaf, dry the slices on a baking sheet in a low oven until they are quite brittle, but not coloured. Pound them to crumbs with a rolling pin, or in the electric blender. To make the stuffing, mix the breadcrumbs with the well-washed parsley, add the grated peel of the two lemons and the strained juice of one. Beat in the eggs, then work in the softened butter. Season very lightly. Stuff the bird (body and crop) and secure the flaps with small metal skewers, so that the stuffing will not burst out during cooking.

Rub the bird with ¼ lb. of butter, putting lumps between the thighs and body. Wrap the bird in cooking foil, also lavishly buttered. Stand the parcel, the turkey lying on its side, on a rack in a baking tin, and place it low down in the oven preheated to very moderate, gas No. 2, 310°F. A bird weighing 12–14 lb. will take approximately three hours to cook. At half time turn the bird over, and thirty minutes before time is up, take away the foil and turn the bird's breast upwards so that it will brown.

GIBLET GRAVY

Two carrots; an onion; a small glass of white wine or vermouth; ½ lb. of stewing veal; a bayleaf and twig of thyme; two tomatoes; the turkey giblets.

The giblet gravy is best started off a day ahead of time. Put the giblets (keep the liver for another dish), the flavouring vegetables, wine, herbs, veal, and halved and grilled tomatoes in a small soup pot over a low flame without other liquid. Let all these ingredients take colour before adding salt and enough water to cover. Transfer the pot, covered, to a very low oven (perhaps at the same time as the bread for the stuffing is drying) for about two hours, and return it to the oven again if there is room while the turkey is cooking. At about the same time as you open the oven to take the foil off the turkey, remove the giblet stock, strain it, transfer it to a saucepan and keep it ready on the top of the stove for the final heating up.

ANGEVIN SALAD

Hearts of two lettuces or of two curly endives or Batavian endives; ½ lb. Gruyère or Emmenthal cheese; olive oil and wine vinegar dressing.

Salad and cheese in one course, i.e. not American but French, and very delicate and unusual. See that the salad is good and crisp (wash and dry it well ahead of time, and store it in a clean cloth in the refrigerator). With it in the bowl mix the Gruyère or Emmenthal (the one with large holes, whereas the real Gruyère has very small ones) cut into tiny cubes. Add the dressing (6 tablespoonfuls of olive oil to a teaspoonful or two of vinegar) at the last minute.

PRUNES IN ARMAGNAC

In South Western France plums or greengages preserved in brandy or Armagnac are served, one or two per person, in small glasses, with a little of the liqueur. A very excellent idea – providing fruit, sweet and liqueur combined. It is feasible to improvise something of the kind for oneself by packing outsize Californian dried prunes into wide glass preserving jars or stoppered sweet jars, covering them with a white dessert wine such as Monbazillac, then adding a good measure of Armagnac or Cognac. Leave for a minimum of three weeks before broaching the jar.

ELIZABETH DAVID

Some Food for Boxing Day

Parson James Woodforde, in his famous *Diary* records ordering for Christmas Day 1773 the following dinner at New College, Oxford. 'Two fine Codds boiled with fryed souls (sic) round them and oyster sauce, a fine sirloin of Beef roasted, some peas soup and Orange Pudding for the first course; for the second we had a lease of Wild Duck roasted, a fore Qu: of Lamb and Sallad and mince pies.'

For 1967 Jean Garrett offered a simple menu for Boxing Day, to counteract the self-indulgence of the previous day. The fish pie and crème caramel could be made on Christmas Eve and stored in the least cold part of the refrigerator. All these recipes are lovely dishes in their own right and would be welcome to the palate before the next few days of cold poultry, plum pudding and mince pies. All are enough for six people.

SPINACH SOUFFLÉ

One large packet Findus chopped spinach, 1 oz. butter, ¾ oz. flour, ¼ pint milk, 2 tablespoonfuls thick cream, salt, pepper and nutmeg. 3 oz. grated cheese, Gruyère and Parmesan, three egg yolks, five egg whites (two from crème caramel), 2 tablespoonfuls crisp breadcrumbs.

Cook spinach according to directions on packet and drain well, Melt butter in same pan as spinach and stir in flour. Pour on milk and cook, stirring for five minutes. Remove pan from heat and add cream, seasonings and cheese. Stir in egg yolks. Just before dinner beat egg whites and fold into spinach mixture. Turn into a prepared dish and dust with breadcrumbs. Cook at gas No. 6, 400°F for about twenty-five minutes. Serve with hot French bread.

FISH PIE

$1\frac{1}{4}$ lb. cooked, flaked fish, half smoked and half fresh haddock, 1 oz. butter, 1 oz. flour, good $\frac{1}{2}$ pint hot milk (infused for ten minutes with a slice of onion and carrot, a blade of mace, a small bayleaf, six peppercorns, some parsley stalks and thyme), 3-4 tablespoonfuls cream, two hard boiled eggs, three large tomatoes, 4 oz. peeled prawns, 1 tablespoonful chopped parsley, 8 oz. puff pastry.

Make a good Béchamel sauce by melting butter in heavy saucepan and stirring in flour. Cook for a few minutes and pour on strained milk. Bring to boil stirring and continue cooking for ten minutes. Stir in cream. Now add fish to the sauce, chopped eggs, peeled, seeded and chopped tomatoes, prawns and parsley. Pour into pie dish and cover with puff pastry suitably decorated and brushed with a little egg. Bake at gas No. 7-8, 425°F for fifteen minutes and reduce heat to No. 4-5 for another fifteen minutes. Serve with salad.

CRÈME CARAMEL

4 oz. granulated sugar, 2 tablespoonfuls water, two eggs, two egg yolks 2 oz. vanilla flavoured caster sugar, 1 pint scalded milk.

In a heavy saucepan melt the sugar in water and cook briskly until a good brown. Pour resulting caramel into six warmed individual soufflé dishes $3\frac{1}{2}$ inches in diameter. Beat whole eggs and yolks with vanilla sugar and pour over them the milk. Strain into the little dishes and set these in a roasting tin half full of warm water. Cover with greaseproof paper and bake for 1 hour at gas No. 2, 300°F. Chill until needed and then carefully turn out.

For other days in December

GRILLED DOUBLE LAMB CHOP

A double chop, a cut invented or at any rate popularized in England in the mid-nineteenth century by Alexis Soyer, the celebrated chef at the Reform Club, is a chop sawn right across the saddle, so that it is really two cutlets joined together by the central bone. Its advantages over the ordinary single neck cutlet is that it has much less tendency to dry up during the cooking and that although it is so quickly and simply cooked it makes a handsome enough dish to take the place of a joint or a bird at a lunch or dinner party.

According to the size and age of the animal from which the double chops have been cut they will weigh between 5 and 8 oz. each. Coat them on each side with a film of olive oil or melted butter in the grill pan put a few sprigs of thyme, put the chops on the top and grill them rather gently, turning them over two or three times, for ten to fifteen minutes according to their weight. Sprinkle each side with salt only when it has been sealed by the heat.

Serve them on a well-heated dish with a little bunch of watercress at each end, some mint butter (very finely chopped mint worked with butter and lemon juice) upon each chop, and a few potatoes separately.

Celery cooked according to the method given in the pheasant recipe below goes admirably with lamb dishes.

SOLE WITH MUSSELS AND WHITE WINE

For one large sole weighing about 1 lb., and skinned on both sides, the other ingredients are 2 pints of mussels, a large onion, a wineglass (about 4 oz.) of dry white wine, 2 oz. of butter, parsley, lemon juice and seasonings.

Heat 1 oz. of butter, in a heavy frying pan and in this cook the finely sliced onion until it is soft and yellow. It should not be browned.

While it is cooking put the scraped and well-washed mussels into a saucepan with the wine, bring to the boil, and as soon as the mussels open remove them from the saucepan with a draining spoon. Filter the liquid through a muslin placed in a sieve.

Spread the cooked onion, well seasoned, in a wide shallow baking dish. On top put the sole. Over it pour enough of the filtered mussel liquid just to come level with it. Cover the dish with foil or a lid and cook in a moderate oven, gas No. 4, 350°F for fifteen minutes.

Meanwhile shell the mussels and chop a tablespoonful of parsley. Work this in to the remaining ounce of butter and add a squeeze of lemon.

Put the shelled mussels round the sole and the parsley butter on top and return to the oven for five minutes, just long enough for the mussels to heat through and for the butter to melt. This will serve only two people, and should you wish to make it in a larger quantity and have only one baking dish of the right size, have two soles filleted and cook them only fifteen minutes altogether. This dish is also excellent with turbot or fillets of John Dory or halibut.

PHEASANT WITH CELERY

For a young and tender roasting pheasant weighing about 8 lb. when drawn and dressed, the rest of the ingredients are 2 oz. of streaky salt pork or mild bacon, 2 oz. butter, a small glass (about 4 oz.) of white wine and a large head of celery plus another ounce of butter and a few drops of olive oil for cooking it.

To cook the pheasant melt 1 oz. butter in a heavy and deepish pot in which the bird will just about fit. Add the diced pork or bacon. Put the second ounce of butter, worked with a little salt and pepper, inside the pheasant, and when the fat from the pork starts to run, put the bird in on its side and let it gently take colour before turning it over and adding the heated wine. Let the wine bubble a few seconds, then turn the heat low, cover the pot, and cook gently for forty to forty-five minutes, turning the bird over at half time.

Have the celery well washed and drained and the strings from the outside sticks scraped off with a sharp knife. Cut into $\frac{1}{2}$-inch chunks. Melt the third ounce of butter and the olive oil in a heavy 10 inch frying pan. Put in the celery, stir it around, sprinkle with a little salt, cover the pan and let it simmer gently for ten minutes. Then take a spoonful of the juices from the bird and add it to the celery. Cook another five minutes, then transfer the celery to the hot serving dish, put the pheasant on top (carve it for serving if it's convenient to do so at this stage) and the little bits of pork all round, and keep the dish covered while you reduce the juices in the pan by fast boiling for a minute or two.

You can now, if you have some brandy, Calvados or Armagnac to spare, add a tablespoonful or two to the sauce; but in this case let it cook a minute or two longer before serving it separately in a sauce boat with the pheasant and celery.

ELIZABETH DAVID

A Valediction
and In Homage

Here are my three farewell dishes, which I have cooked with consistent success, thanks to Elizabeth David's recipes and faultless instructions. Two of them are extravagant, because, alas, both lobster and fillet of beef are expensive. But they are perfection of their kind, and simple to prepare. Each recipe is for four people.

HOMARD A LA CRÈME

Two small cooked lobsters, $\frac{1}{4}$ lb. mushrooms, 4 oz. cream, one liquer glass each brandy and pale dry sherry, 2 oz. butter, lemon juice, salt and pepper, cayenne pepper.

Melt the butter in a shallow pan and put in the pieces of lobster, seasoned with the salt, pepper and lemon juice. When the butter is foaming, pour in the brandy and set it alight, and as soon as it has finished burning add the mushrooms thinly sliced the sherry and a touch of cayenne. Stir for two to three minutes and pour in the cream. Another five minutes and the lobster is ready.

This is a simple dish, too often spoilt by the addition of tomato sauce, too much sherry and a thickening of flour and milk. The sherry must be of finest quality.

CHATEAUBRIAND EN TERRINE

Into an earthenware terrine with a lid pour a wine glass of dry white vin ordinaire, a wine glass of Bual Madeira, and a liqueur glass of brandy, and put this to heat gently on a low flame.

Now slice two or three small onions, the same number of carrots, and sauté them very lightly in butter. In the same butter sauté on each side your beef, which should be a fine quality piece of fillet, thick and in one piece, seasoned with salt and pepper.

By this time the contents of the terrine should just be beginning to simmer; place the beef in this liquid, cover it with the carrots and onions, and add a chopped shallot, a suspicion of garlic, four fine tomatoes, peeled, and each cut into eight pieces.

Now cover the terrine and seal the lid with a flour and water paste. Place the terrine in a very slow oven (No. 1–2) for two hours. Serve in the dish in which it has cooked and accompany, if you like, with a very light purée of potatoes.

COFFEE CHESTNUTS

For four people you need about thirty-six shelled and skinned chestnuts. Put them in a pan with enough water to cover and 2 tablespoonfuls of sugar. Simmer until soft. In another pan, preferably a double saucepan, put the yolks of two eggs, a tablespoonful of sugar, a teacupful of strong black coffee and a liqueur glass of rum. Stir over a low flame until it thickens and pour it over the strained chestnuts in a silver dish.

Index of recipes

A selection of books

LADY ARABELLA BOXER: *First Slice Your Cookbook*, Nelson
MICHAEL BROADBENT: *Wine Tasting*,
    Wine and Spirit Publications
ELIZABETH DAVID: *A Book of Mediterranean Food*, Penguin
French Country Cooking, Penguin
French Provincial Cooking, Penguin
Summer Cooking, Penguin
HUGH JOHNSON: *Wine*, Nelson
SIR ROBERT BRUCE LOCKHART: *Scotch*, Putnam
DR EDOUARD DE POMIANE: *Cooking in Ten Minutes*, Faber
Cooking with Pomiane, Faber
PAMELA VANDYKE PRICE: *Wine Lovers' Handbook*,
    Condé Nast & Collins
CYRIL RAY editor: *The Gourmet's Companion*, Eyre & Spottiswoode
ALLAN SICHEL: *Wines*, Penguin